LEFT FOR DEAD

Nadia Kaci
Rahmouna Salah
Fatiha Maamoura

Left for dead

The Lynching of the Women of Hassi Messaoud

Max Milo
Témoignage

Max Milo Éditions, Paris, 2023
www.maxmilo.com
ISBN : 978-2-31501-252-7

Friday, July 13, 2001

Three hundred to five hundred men passed on the message. The punitive expedition ordered by the imam of El Haïcha would take place tonight. The day before, at the mosque, he had finally given them the green light.

For a long time now, he had been pointing an accusing finger at these fornicators, carriers of AIDS and other diseases. They were taking the work of simple, modest men; they were arousing their sinful urges by strutting naked (without hijabs*) all over town; they were soiling the reputation of their humble neighborhoods; and they were drawing the wrath of Allah!*

We had to crack down, teach them a lesson. Show these whores their place, their only place. The one demanded by their sex. Wanted by tradition. Ordered by Allah.

We had to be fierce to finally get them to respect their rank and play their roles!

- You must purify every street in our city! Allah is with you! Holy war in the name of God! he proclaimed before retreating.

The men decided to "purify" the three main districts of their city.
The two-hundred-housing district, the one-hundred-and-thirty-six-housing district and El Haïcha, officially named Bouamama.
It was in the latter neighborhood that there were the most women.

They met at the entrance to the two hundred...

... armed with clubs, sticks, knives or sabres. Armed with all the hatred they'd been inculcated with for these women. Determined to prove to them, to themselves, their supremacy. Determined to take revenge for all the frustrations their mere presence aroused and fuelled.

- Allahou akbar! El Djihad fi sabil Allah! God is great! Holy war in the name of God!

That was the signal for departure.

With their blood boiling, they threw flaming tires into the middle of the road to prevent anyone from coming to the women's aid.

In the distance, a man waved a gray shirt in his hand. He was calling to them.

Like hungry wolves, they pounced on their first victim.

1. Childhood at the Foot of the Hill

My name is Rahmouna Salah.

I was born on July 12, 1966 in Oran. We were seven children. Five girls and two boys. The eldest, my sister Baya, was nine years older than me. She was like a little mother to us. My brother, Youssef, was two years younger. He didn't talk to me much, but whenever my father wasn't around, he often beat me. My sisters, Khadidja, Fatéma and Nafissa, were five, four and two years younger than me. Discreet and submissive, they obeyed Youssef and never contradicted him. But my favorite was my brother Abdelhak, two years my senior. My lifelong accomplice.

My father was a horse dealer and co-owner of a slaughterhouse. He was a handsome man, quite tall. His fair complexion earned him the nickname *errougi*, meaning "ginger", even though he didn't have a single red hair on his head. *Zahouani*, a notorious party-goer, he adored music and *cheikhates*, the renowned *raï* singers of western Algeria.

We lived in a pleasant little house next to my paternal grandparents', on a quiet street at the foot of a hill. We only saw my father two or three days a week. The rest of his time was divided between his two other wives - of whose existence we children were unaware - and parties. But despite his absences, he made sure we never lacked for anything.

When he went out, he liked one of his daughters to accompany him, as long as she wasn't over pre-pubescent age. When she did, she was replaced by a younger girl. I loved it when he took me to see his friends, especially the women. I thought they were pretty. I remember one of them, who must have been a nurse. We used to visit her in hospital. She wore a beautiful white blouse that highlighted the sparkle of her teeth. She laughed loudly and teased my father a lot. They joked all the time. It amused me enormously. My innocent eyes couldn't understand the true nature of their relationship. But she was probably one of my father's other two wives.

And then there were those night-time jaunts out into the middle of nowhere: on the occasion of a wedding or christening, my father and his friends would get together; I was the only child. We were lit by a huge wood fire around which *sheikhs* and *sheikhates* sang, accompanied by a *gusba* - a wooden flute - and a *bendir*. Dancers swayed to the rhythm of the music. My father forbade me to wander off. I'd fall asleep right next to him, a few meters from the fire, surrounded by the joyful sounds. I liked that.

I didn't like accompanying him to the slaughterhouse. The smell of blood turned my stomach. And those animals we were going to kill, I always refused to go near them. Frozen with fear, I could hear them on the other side of the wall, bellowing their death throes. I've always hated beef.

I loved my father more than anything.

My mother didn't like me following him around. She thought he was too permissive with his daughters. He was always saying:
- They'll do what they want.
- They'll go to school if they feel like it.
- They will marry the man of their choice.

For her part, she grumbled all day long:
- It's your father who will lose you.
- Follow your father and you'll see, he'll lead you to your ruin.
- If you dishonor me, you're no longer my daughter!
- If you embarrass me, I'll suck your blood!
She never sucked anyone's blood. But her little phrases were painful to hear, even if I didn't understand them all. I felt they were full of possible hatred.

I was less attached to Ma[1] because she wasn't very patient with us. In her defense, she was very tired. Most of the time, she was pregnant, and her pregnancies were always difficult. As for childbirth, it was particularly painful for her. She lost a lot of blood. Sometimes her babies. Seven died at birth or in infancy. I remember one of my brothers. Mahmoud. Tiny. Agonizing in his bed. His belly swollen. I watched him go, helpless and sad to see Ma cry.

My brothers also hit me. On the pretext that I didn't eat at the same time as everyone else, that I was too cheeky, that I talked back; or because I had disobeyed my mother, preferring to go for a walk with my father. I think they were jealous: my father would never ask one of his sons to join him. So they beat me. When Dad came back, I'd complain. He'd hit them, and then when Dad left, my brothers would hit me again, because I'd complained to my father.

However, I never resented my brother Abdelhak for very long. After all, when I wasn't feeling well, only he would notice. What's more, he was my only playmate. We shared the same room and were inseparable. When he caught pneumonia at the age of 8, I caught it too. The illness isolated us from the rest of the family. We

---

1. In Oranie, as in many parts of the Maghreb, mom is called "Ma".

were hospitalized for three months. When we got out, we were told we'd missed the start of the school year. It was heartbreaking for me: I'd been looking forward to it so much! My father decided to enroll us both in a private school eight kilometers from our home. His driver drove us in the morning and picked us up at the end of the day.

One day, my father gave us a sumptuous gift. A little red car that we could both ride in. We'd pull it up to the top of the hill. And race down the street, laughing like mad. We never wanted to leave it. So much so that one morning, as the driver was waiting to take us to school, my brother asked me:

- Go see Dad. He'll listen to you. Tell him you're sick. Then we can stay home and play with our car.

I agreed, because I liked the idea so much. But my father wasn't fooled:

- You're not sick," he said. Here's some change. Buy yourself some candy and run off to school.

- But Dad, they'll steal the car if we leave it here.

- I'll put it on the terrace. Scram!

- I'm really sick. I don't want to go.

My father grabbed me violently between his strong arms and threw me to the sidewalk. I leapt to my feet, shouting:

- I'm healed, Daddy! I'm healed. I'm going to school!

That was the only time he hit me, but I was sore for three days.

On another occasion, we found a baby bird that had fallen from its nest. It looked very fragile, but it was alive. My brother said to me:

- If we don't take him with us, he'll die. Put it in your schoolbag. We'll make him a little nest with our socks. That way, he'll make it all the way home. There, we'll take care of him until he grows up.

I refused. Our mistress was far too strict, and I didn't dare imagine her reaction and the punishment that would follow if she discovered the animal.

- If she sees it, I'll explain that I put it in your schoolbag," my brother assured me.

Shortly after arriving at the classroom, little plaintive cries escaped from my bag and propelled the teacher straight at me. Her wooden ruler, which never left her side, persuaded me quickly enough:

- It was my brother's idea to put this little bird in my schoolbag. I had nothing to do with it.

- I didn't even know the baby bird was in his schoolbag," Abdelhak retorted without batting an eyelid.

I should have known: as with the cakes he'd sent me to steal from my mother's dresser, he denied everything, without scruple. I received ten blows on my fingers. When I got out of school, mad with rage, I grabbed a big rock and hit my brother on the head. I hit him once. There was a lot of blood.

But the next day, we were back to being the best of friends.

2. Tata Zakia

Aunt Zakia didn't live very far from the school. So at lunchtime, when it was cold, we would go and have lunch at her house. This meant we didn't have to waste time travelling home. And we could play with her son, who was about our age. Ma said it calmed her down to know we were at Aunt Zakia's.

Aunt Zakia wasn't really our aunt. But since my maternal uncle was keen to marry her, she was already part of the family. Except that she was already married. She had made the pilgrimage to Mecca, which earned her the honorary title of *hadja*. She wasn't very pretty, but she had charisma and glibness. She also had beautiful jewelry and lots of gold teeth. She owned a herd of sheep and oxen, and had gone into business with my maternal uncles to increase her capital. She came to visit us regularly; one afternoon, my father arrived unannounced and was not pleased to find her in the main room. He reproached my mother for her bad company and made her promise not to see her again. Ma, usually obedient to her husband, was unable to keep this promise: the rules of hospitality did not allow her to.

Auntie Zakia had a strange habit. Every time she visited, she proposed a new marriage:

- I'd take you for my nephew. He'll make you beautiful children and you'll want for nothing," she once told my eldest sister.

- *Hadja*, I'm 15. I'm a little young to get married.

- Yes, but very soon you'll be old. So think fast, because he's old enough and he won't wait for you.

Another day, it was to my uncle Ahmed, my mother's little brother, that she said:

- If you want, I'll give you my niece. She's young and pretty. What's more, you'll be guaranteed a certificate of virginity.

Uncle Ahmed agreed.

One day, people told my mother that Aunt Zakia might have been Dad's mistress.

- You see," replied my mother calmly, "my husband has many conquests, that's a fact. But why should he be interested in this woman who's married, *hadja*, older than him and, let's face it, not very pretty? Let me stop you right there. My husband will never look at that woman.

The incident was over.

But one lunchtime, as Abdelhak and I entered Aunt Zakia's house, I noticed a strangely familiar plaid jacket in her vestibule:

- Auntie Zakia, isn't that Daddy's jacket?" I asked.

- That's my husband Djelloul's jacket. They must have the same one, that's all.

- I don't think your husband could afford such a lovely jacket.

Her husband worked for the commune.

That evening, at dinner, I asked my father:

- Were you at Auntie Zakia's today?

- No," he replied without batting an eyelid.

- In any case, your jacket was there.

My mother's face turned white. At night, we heard them arguing.

A few days later, Dad opened Aunt Zakia's door for us at lunchtime. He tried to get me to keep his secret: he promised me a dress and sunglasses, like Egyptian actresses, if I kept quiet. He also promised to break my jaw if I talked.

I reported it to my sister, who passed it on to my mother, who immediately went to see Zakia's husband.

- Impossible," he told her. My wife is as ugly as a louse. Your husband is handsome and rich. He can do much better.

- Open your eyes! I'm telling you that my husband is taking your wife home. And you're telling me your wife is as ugly as a louse?! You should hang yourself instead of spouting such nonsense!

Everyone thought Zakia had bewitched my father.

And then things accelerated.

Screams, punches and kicks were a regular occurrence. My father beat my mother frequently. As if he didn't want her to exist anymore. As if he wanted us to disappear. Her body and face swollen, in the throes of her fifteenth pregnancy, she wandered around the house, enraged, exhausted...

One day he came home and didn't speak. He just banged and banged. My mother didn't even scream anymore. She was like a rag doll in his hands. My grandfather jumped up and tried to intervene. He shouted:

- Stop this! You're possessed!

We, too, tried to fight his blind hatred, to block it with our bodies. We shouted, desperate and terrified. Then Dad went away again, just like that. Ma was bathed in a great pool of blood. Big black clots were coming out from between her thighs.

Ma was hospitalized for several days. I prayed she wouldn't die.

Dad reappeared. He groaned, he didn't understand what had come over him. He was sorry. Ma would come home from the hospital with a baby. Very cute, for sure.

Dad, I didn't recognize him anymore.

Ma lost twins six months into her pregnancy.

And Dad did it again.

One evening, on the way home from school, my father strangled my mother with a *chèche*[2]. My brothers and sisters tried to separate them. But Dad held firm. He bellowed:

- Today I kill you. Today is your day!

My mother was no longer conscious. My father continued to squeeze. Grandpa rushed to our house. He said to me:

- Crawl between his legs and bite his hand!

Dad let go of Ma and ran off.

He never came home again.

Later, we learned that Auntie Zakia had sent her husband to pick olives on her land. When he returned, the house was empty. Not a piece of furniture left. Dad and Auntie Zakia had hired a truck to take everything away.

My mother took me to court for the divorce decree. That's when I realized that all the love I'd felt for him had turned to hate.

My mother said:

- Judge, this woman took my husband away from me and left me with seven children.

Auntie Zakia's husband said:

- Judge, this man took my wife and son and gutted my house!

---

2. Piece of cloth worn wrapped around the head or neck.

The judge looked weary and said:
- I'm not going to take them home by force, so why don't you tell us what your requests are and get it over with!
Alimony has been fixed.
My father only paid her if the bailiffs intervened.

My eldest brother had to leave for military service. There were no men left at home. In our family, women don't work. A matter of honor. Especially as we had a reputation for being well-to-do. So my mother used to say:
- God will provide for us.
In the meantime, she sold her gold and spent what little savings she had left. My maternal uncles helped as best they could, but our situation was deteriorating. Ma didn't want to show anything, but the furniture in the house was disappearing one by one.
We had to leave school. Abdelhak was sent to train as a mechanic and I was sent home. I must have been about 11 or 12.
And then, as the years went by, things began to stabilize. Baya was married. Her husband, Miloud, always present, always pleasant, also supported us. Youssef came back and started working. We were already living better.
My mother was even able to travel to Mecca thanks to her brothers. It was her dearest wish.

2. Tata Zakia

I was 17 at the time.

When the pilgrims returned, as we didn't live far from the airport and plane delays were long, family members came to wait for their loved ones at our place. I had to take care of all these people by preparing food for them. According to my brother Youssef's wishes, who loved to entertain, the meal had to be a small feast.

Among our guests was one of my mother's cousins. He was waiting for his father. He was an educated man who had studied in Saudi Arabia. He wore a beautiful suit. And shoes so shined you could see yourself in them. He was 27 and his name was Mourad.

3. Mourad

We ended up seeing him more and more often at home. Until one day, he asked me to marry him. He wasn't a bad guy. But I wasn't attracted to him at all. His slicked-back head to straighten his frizzy hair and his superior airs annoyed me.

I refused.

He didn't like my answer at all. He swore at me, his face contorted with contempt and hatred:

- I'll marry you whether you like it or not.

My elder sister arrived that evening with her husband. Youssef, Abdelhak and my mother were also there. We couldn't understand why I refused such a good match. Ma exclaimed that she wouldn't dare look into the eyes of Mourad's mother, one of the family members for whom she had the most respect. My sister said I'd never get another chance like this. I shouted that he wasn't to my liking.

- You think you're in Switzerland telling us that! If someone tells you to marry him, you marry him and don't argue!" Youssef told me.

Only Abdelhak defended me:

- But if she doesn't want to get married, we can't force her.

- Start by working! How do you like a house full of girls?! She's getting married, because we've decided. The others will follow and there won't be a girl left! Off you go!

Abdelhak, my ally, had run out of arguments against the marriage. I couldn't blame him, he wasn't in a strong position.

Annoyed, I bowed to their will.

The two families met at our house. All my mother's conditions regarding the dowry were accepted. My uncle, happy, joined me in the bedroom and kissed me to congratulate me. I fainted. I wanted to die. But suicide is forbidden in our religion. Besides, I would have hurt Ma too much.

Some time later, I had to go to my father's house to ask for a marriage license, since I was still a minor. I hoped he would take the opportunity to ask me if I was all right and, above all, if I was willing.

But he just mumbled:

- And what's more, she's found you a husband in her family.

He refused, because he didn't care about us anymore. I was furious.

- Everything you've done to Ma, everything you've done to us, I'll make you regret later, when I'm older! I promise.

The judge agreed that Youssef could give his consent in his place.

The wedding took place in 1985. On the wedding night, Mourad exclaimed:

- If you're not a virgin, I'll send you back to your mother.

This sentence stabbed me in the heart and made my blood run cold. We had provided her family with two certificates of virginity. The first, at the time of the engagement. The second, after a visit to the gynecologist the day before. And that wasn't enough?

He had married me against my will, when I was a minor, and threatened to send me away if I didn't prove I was a virgin. How could I love him?

A few days later, as I was breaking in a make-up bag given to me by my sister, he announced the color of our common future: no make-up, waxing, hairdressing, outings or visits. No Western TV either. Everything was *h'ram*. Forbidden by our religion.

He was also jealous. Even of his nephew, who must have been 16, he forbade me to speak to him. A man, whether my brother or brother-in law, could only visit me in his presence. After each of his visits to his mother's house, he would return, aggressive and suspicious. I had no choice but to forbid the women in my family access to the house if he wasn't there.

I took it upon myself to convince myself that this was my destiny.

Despite this, he criticized me all the time: the dishes I cooked were either too salty or not salty enough. The furniture wasn't in the right place. His uniform was badly ironed. One day, I exploded:

- Your uniform, you can bring my mother, your mother, my sister, my brother, whoever you want, this is the last time I'll iron it. Go up to heaven and come down next time and iron it yourself.

The arguments were incessant, and her mother was always getting in the way. This woman, who looked like a marabout, dressed all in white, respected by the whole family, the neighbors and everyone who came across her, was my worst nightmare.

I was soon overcome by nausea. I thought it was the effect Mourad was having on me, the physical and moral exhaustion. But it turned out I was pregnant. His mother practically moved in with us. She spied on my every move, belittled me and insulted me. Living with them became insurmountable.

And as my pregnancy progressed, it turned out to be a real illness, with endless vomiting and dizziness.

At six months, I lost my baby. I was relieved. I didn't want to go back to my husband, I hoped that my mother and brothers would take me in, that I'd get back to some semblance of normal life I was so nostalgic for my childhood home!

But they turned me down. Once again, I had to resign myself.

Shortly afterwards, I became pregnant again. This announcement made Mourad happy. He gave me a pair of slippers. It was the first present he'd given me since we got married. He said I had to stop walking barefoot all day long. Otherwise the cold would get into my belly through my feet:

- That's why you lost our first child," he asserted.

Vomiting and nausea began to plague my life again. But that wasn't all. Mourad harassed me again and again under the pretext of educating me. My life was a real ordeal and I was afraid of losing my child again. When I was six months pregnant, I told him:

- We stop everything!

Seeing my condition, my mother accepted my return this time.

4. Repudiation Times Three

One torrential rainy evening, I heard a noise in the courtyard. It was Mourad. He was crying his eyes out.

My mother tried to calm him down:

- When she's had the baby, when she's better, she'll come back. And you'll be nicer to her, and that'll be that.

But he was crying harder.

- Are you stupid or what to cry for a woman!" exclaimed my mother.

- Yes, my cousin," he replied, "I'm a fool because I repudiated her!

- Too bad for you, it'll be worth the price of a party, because you'll marry her again and she can come back," retorted my mother.

- No, my cousin. She can never come back, because I've repudiated her three times," he moaned through his sobs. It was my mother who pushed me over the edge.

Ma brought her into the house. She was crying too:

- Her brother didn't want her around before she got married, and he's not going to accept her now that she's expecting a child. You could have waited until she gave birth. You would have taken her child away from her, she would have had no choice but to follow him. I should never have agreed to your marriage.

Still in tears, Mourad came to get me.

- Gather your things, we're going home.

My mother took offense:

- But you want her to live in sin?

- I'll find a solution.

I followed him, feeling really sorry for him.

He asked all the imams in Algeria for advice. They all had the same version: "After a repudiation not three times, you can no longer remarry together, unless the woman consummates a marriage with another man and then divorces him."

He hadn't shaved for two months. He was so unhappy that it moved me. Why hadn't he shown me his love before, instead of trying to "check me out"? Despite our official separation, we slept in the same room. It was with this man of too much faith that I was forced to live in sin.

- You see, it's not possible. No imam will agree to remarry us. It's better that we separate. I'm handing everything over to you," I finally told him. I signed the divorce consent papers.

His mother had already chosen another wife for him. He called me every day to see how I was, to make sure I had everything I needed. Even on his wedding day. And then for two days, nothing.

That's when my baby decided to be born.

5. Hamid, My Son

The contractions tore at my belly and the pain reverberated throughout the rest of my body. Just as the head was about to come out, I felt a searing pain: my flesh was being cut raw with a blade. An episiotomy. Without anaesthetic, as the products were in short supply.

At midnight, a beautiful 5.1-kilo baby came out of my womb.

I stayed in the operating room to get stitches. I was fainting, so intolerable was the operation for my body, which was already a gaping wound. The members of the nursing team revived me, waiting for me to regain my strength. They themselves tried to recover, resting their heads on the edge of my bed. Then they'd start all over again, and I'd feel the needle prick me and the thread penetrate my aching flesh, digging in and being pulled out. Childbirth had exposed all the nerves in my belly. They finished suturing me at 4 o'clock in the morning. We were all exhausted.

In the morning, I asked a nurse to bring my little one back to me. At last, I held my child in my arms. He was beautiful. His calmness impressed me. He, too, had had a few stitches in his skull: the doctors had injured him during the episiotomy. He must have suffered as violently as his mother, poor darling. His fragility touched me. Yet he didn't cry, didn't ask for his milk.

The idea that his father's absence would follow him all his life, that he wouldn't have a real home because his maternal uncle wouldn't hear of him, hurt. What would become of us? He slept soundly, as if sensing the need to regain his strength for what was to come. I promised him I would never abandon him.

Never. Ever. Ever.

Mourad had told my sister that if it was a boy, he wanted to call him Hamid. He was so uninterested in the idea of a girl that he didn't come up with a name. So we named him Hamid.

My brother-in-law Miloud decided that, given the care we were receiving in hospital, it would be better to leave that evening: I'd be better looked after at home.

Youssef, who was having dinner in the kitchen, didn't get up when I entered, supported by Baya and my mother. My sister showed him Hamid:

- Look how beautiful our little angel is! Would you like to give him a hug?

- Get that bastard out of my sight," he muttered.

Only my mother, who at the time still had the strength to stand up to him, dared to threaten him:

- I hope you never have boys and that your daughters go through what you're doing to mine. Rahmouna is at home. If you're not happy, it's up to you to get your things.

Back home, we often say, "Beware the prayers of angry mothers." I don't know if this has anything to do with it, but my brother, much to his regret, never had boys.

The mother-in-law came at the end of the day. She wouldn't let go of my baby. He had already been aspirated at the hospital, but she made him scream by repeating the operation.

A little later, Dad arrived with his arms full of presents.

Everyone was gathered in the room. He crossed it without greeting anyone. He kissed me, which was against all the rules, took his son in his arms and started crying, crying, sobbing. His child clutched him tightly. He reproached his mother:

- You're the one depriving me of my son.

Then he kissed his baby.

- You're depriving him of growing up in a family with a mom and dad. You're depriving my son of his father," he complained.

5. Hamid, My Son

I didn't know whether to laugh or cry. I quickly chose my side when the mother-in-law retorted in her husky necromancer voice:

- Wasn't it agreed that she would hand the child over to us at birth?

To make sure I could get away from them, I had indeed made this promise. It didn't matter if it was a lie to free me from their shackles, or if I really meant it at the time; in my defense, the immature young woman I was was not yet aware, at the time, that the child she carried in her womb was real. And now that he was in my arms, my breast in his mouth, and his scent on my skin, it was out of the question!

For two days and nights, they stayed at home. They tried to convince me to leave Hamid with them. Each had his own arguments. She said:

- You're young. If you give us the child, you'll be able to remarry more easily. Even if you're not a virgin. On the other hand, who's going to want a child that isn't his?

He demanded that I separate from my son as soon as possible, so that I wouldn't get too attached to him and his second wife could raise and mother him like her own baby. In desperation, he suggested I move in with them to raise him.

Ma was beginning to find the time long. She closed the discussion:

- We don't take children away from their mothers. Even though you've been unfair to my daughter, we don't dispute that you're still the boy's father. You can come and see him as much as you like. He'll visit you for vacations and vacations, if you like. But his home will be where his mother lives, and nowhere else.

I discovered Ma in a different light. Supportive and loving. I was extremely grateful.

Mourad and his mother did try to get Hamid back through the courts by trying to smear me. But it didn't work.

And in my childhood home, everyone surrounded my son with sweet words and love.

6. Faïçal, My Second Marriage

When my son was 2, I received another marriage proposal.

I was with my aunt in a bakery. Hamid was repeating at the top of his lungs:

- Ma, cakes, Ma, cakes!

I loved spoiling him. Seeing him happy always filled me with joy. The handsome young man who served us, we later learned, was the bakery's co-owner. Of average height, he had a lovely tanned complexion and beautiful hands.

- Husband can't be far away, with such a lovely family," he complimented us with a beautiful smile that revealed perfect teeth.

- The husband is very far away, because unfortunately my niece is divorced.

- So young! What a shame," exclaimed the young man.

Embarrassed, I walked out and let them continue their palaver.

A few days later, we saw him arrive with a big box of cakes. He talked to my brothers and uncles:

- I asked around about Rahmouna. I'm told she's a serious girl. I'm willing to marry her. I'm willing to look after her child as if it were my own. But there will be conditions: I'll be the only one to decide for her. There's no question of her working or even leaving the house. If she wants to go to the hammam, I'll go with her. If she wants to visit her mother, I'll go with her. If she wants to go to the doctor, I'll do the same. As for the rest, there's no reason for her to set foot outside the house.

Everyone thought it was harsh. Even my brother Youssef, whom my first marriage had perhaps given pause for thought, urged me to turn down the proposal.

I accepted it: whether they or he decided for me, what difference did it make?

What's more, my dear Abdelhak had once told me that a woman who had been repudiated, no matter how young, could only remarry an old man. This shocked me: the idea of sharing my life with a senile old man as a husband oppressed and despaired me to no end. Faïçal was my chance to escape this horrible fate and, above all, he offered to look after my son as if he were his own. What other man in our society would do that? My little Hamid would no longer feel fatherless. For me, that was the most important thing.

I wanted this wedding to be beautiful and happy. It wasn't grandiose, but we organized it with care. And this time, I participated wholeheartedly.

On January 10, 1988, the day of the ceremony, as tradition dictates, we planned a big party at my mother's house before my husband took me home.

Ma came into the room while I was getting ready.

- Girl, I think you're cursed. Your ex-husband is in the courtyard with the guests. He's got Hamid in his arms and he's crying in his lap.

- But Ma, you're the one who got in my way," I reminded her before leaving the room.

I took Mourad aside:

- Why are you doing this to me on my wedding day?

- I didn't want it to be like this. My second wife left. I was ready to get you back with or without repudiation three times over.

- And you've made up your mind just on the day I'm getting married...? please don't make a fuss. No one will accept our marriage anyway.

- Then at least give me my son. You'll have others. But I have nothing left.

- I can't do it. Be patient. Your mother will find you a wife in no time.

Faïçal was furious. I understood him. This was our day.

- We can't deny him access to our house. He's my mother's cousin and her child lives here," I tried to explain.

By way of reply, he started to push me around. Then he took a deep breath to calm himself:

- Get your things, we're leaving now.

I wasn't ready, as it was customary to leave for my husband's house at the end of the day. My mother arranged for us to leave as soon as possible. She said to me:

- I can't go with you while your ex-husband's here. Your sisters will come with you.

That night, Mourad slept at my mother's with the other guests. His son next to him.

Faïçal was kind, gentle, attentive and pleasant to me for the first thirty days of our union. Then things started to go wrong. He suddenly started talking badly to me, considering that I didn't know how to respond as a wife should to her husband. He was going to teach me, he kept saying. He began to raise his hand to me. First occasionally, then more and more often. I couldn't figure him out: often, after slapping me on the head in correction, he'd come back to me looking jovial and relaxed, as if nothing had happened.

For me, it was more complicated to adopt the same attitude. I was afraid of it. But I consoled myself with the thought that an occasional slap on the roof for my son wasn't such a big deal. And my constant humiliations didn't stop me from considering Faïçal a good father to Hamid. What else could I hope for? Going

39

out would have done me good, of course, but in the end, I didn't care. I had far too much to do with the house and my little one. However, I preferred to take precautions and start my first pack of pills as soon as I was slapped in the face, despite his pressure to have a child as soon as possible.

As I tried my best to respond appropriately to my husband, I learned that I was pregnant. I was told the news at the hospital where I had gone because of abnormal bleeding and because I was vomiting blood.

It was a shock. I'd been on the pill until 1989, and within the first month of stopping it, poof! a pregnancy! I was devastated. The idea of being permanently linked to this man and his violence terrified me.

This second child proved extremely difficult to bear: I was hospitalized until the fifth month, with Valium as my companion and several miscarriage alerts.

7. My Daughters, Nacéra and Hassina

When I gave birth in November, I suffered a hemorrhage that almost took my life. The nurse announced the birth of my daughter to Faïçal; we had agreed that he would bring me home for dinner that evening, but he didn't reappear until two days later. When he did, he made his displeasure clear: how could I have given him a daughter? I hadn't done a good job.

Yet she was beautiful, my daughter. We called her Nacéra: victorious. And despite his initial rejection, Faïçal gradually became attached to her. They often played together, much to my delight.

As Nacéra grew older, minor squabbles broke out between her and her brother. Faïçal began to beat Hamid more and more often. Unfairly.

- Brothers and sisters argue," I tried to calmly reason with my husband. It's not serious, it's their age. There's no need to beat Hamid. Just tell him or scold him.

- No, I want to put him in his place," he retorted wickedly.

And each time, he hit him harder.

Why was this? Was my son out of place?

Faïçal started hitting me more and more frequently, and I started hitting him too.

In 1992, I was pregnant again. The shock was more terrible than the previous time. Having another child with him could only spell doom for our future. God forgive me, I swallowed all the medicines and herbal teas that could induce an abortion. I jumped rope countless times. I jumped off the kitchen table for an entire afternoon, but it was no use. It just hung there. It's a trait I recognize in her today. May she forgive me.

I had the same symptoms and treatments as my first daughter: injections and Valium to protect me from miscarriage.

In my eighth month of pregnancy, I was visited by my paternal aunt and my little cousin, who must have been 17 at the time. I brought out the coffee and cakes to welcome them. After they'd left, I took great care to clean everything up to erase even the smallest trace of their passage. Unfortunately, my little cousin, in his quest for self-assertion, had been smoking; Faïçal, on his return, smelled it. He didn't ask me. He took his daughter aside and asked her:

- Who came to the house?

Nacéra, 3 years old, replied innocently:

- Auntie Chafika and Uncle Kaddour.

Sitting in the courtyard where I was rolling the couscous, I suddenly felt a huge shock on my face. He'd just given me a powerful kick with one of his beautiful black pointy shoes, the ones whose heels he loved to click as he walked.

Faïçal accompanied me to the hospital. I was referred to the ophthalmology department. My eye was shattered. Faïçal wouldn't let go of me.

- Who did this to you?" the doctor asked.

I didn't reply.

- I'll give you a certificate of twenty-one days' incapacity.

- I don't work," I said.

- You don't work, but you can go to the police station and lodge a complaint against the person who did this to you.

He spoke only to me, as if he'd understood everything. He only turned back to Faïçal to say:

- Here's a prescription. Go buy her medicine.

He complied without flinching.

The doctor's reaction, which seemed to empathize with me, gave me a little boost of energy. I ran to the photographer's to take some portraits I could use as evidence, and hurried back.

Back home, once again in Faïçal's grip, I was in the grip of great despair. I wanted to die.

A few weeks later, I gave birth to my third child. The labor was just as painful and complicated as with the previous two; and, as it was still a girl, Faïçal's reaction was almost as violent as with Nacéra.

- You didn't bless God when you had your first daughter, so God is giving you a second one so you can learn to bless Him," I said.

My little princess, Hassina, was born with a deformity in her legs, probably due to Valium. The doctors explained to me that this was treated at Mostaganem hospital. I didn't wait for Faïçal to come with me, or even for him to authorize me to go.

She was six days old when we started massaging her. Braces surrounded her legs until her first birthday. It was worth it: she recovered completely.

8. Low Blows

The slaps rained down, no matter what I said to Faïçal from then on.

After an argument, I took my children to spend a few days with my mother. Mourad took the opportunity to drop in unexpectedly to spend some time with his son. Dreading Faïçal's arrival, I went out to watch on the doorstep.

He was there.

The national sport of neighbors being to spy on their neighbors, he had been easily tipped off.

He tried to hit me, but my mother got in the way. I had to return home with the children. No matter how much I tried to justify my ex-husband's presence at my mother's house, he wouldn't budge.

In the evening, as I was trying to take my mind off sewing my daughters' little dresses, he called me a bitch.

- Bitches only marry dogs," I said.

And wham. Scissors! And so well stuck that my mother, whom I'd called to the rescue, couldn't get them out. She had to take me to the emergency room to have them removed.

When the stitches hadn't yet fallen out, I was visited by a policeman who, with a summons, wanted me to follow him to the police station to answer a complaint lodged by my husband. Climbing into the salad basket in front of all the neighbors, like a criminal, was out of the question. Within a minute, the whole neighborhood and town would know about it. I promised to join him within the hour. This delay also allowed me to collect all my papers. At the police station, when I read the report, I was stunned: he was accusing me of adultery, supported by the obviously false testimony of our immediate neighbors.

I was terribly ashamed in front of the police, for whom anyone entering a police station is necessarily suspect. I wrote my own report.

In court, during the ensuing investigation, the judge (or perhaps the prosecutor, I can't remember exactly), after hearing Faïçal's side of the story, listened to my version. I explained that the man accused of being my lover was my ex-husband and the father of my eldest son; that he was my mother's cousin and that, consequently, it was impossible for me to forbid him to visit his child, since the law itself ordered me to do so.

As for the neighbors, they had agreed to perjure themselves because of a small piece of land that lay between our house and theirs; at one point, they had demanded that we cede it to them in its entirety, even though we were entitled to half. I suspected my husband had promised them the plot in return.

I also showed the state of my back.

- Mr. Prosecutor, if I'd had an extramarital affair, he'd have slit my throat before I set foot in your courtroom," I concluded.

My word has not been questioned.

- What are you asking for in compensation for these slanderous accusations?

- I'm not asking for anything except a divorce.

The public prosecutor then suggested I file for divorce in court.

In the meantime, I returned to my marital home.

9. Divorce

My father fell ill.

Auntie Zakia had abandoned him, finding him too whiny. So he turned to my older sister and me for help. Without resentment, we accompanied him to each of his three hospitalizations. We prepared his meals, took care of his laundry; my mother even washed him.

When he returned from his last hospitalization, Faïçal accompanied the children and me to our parents' house so that we could spend the night there and I could take care of him. The next morning, very early, I got up to go home.

- Stay," begged my sister, "my husband will accompany us later.

- No, I'd rather go home.

The idea of arriving late and angering Faïçal terrified me. I took Hassina in my arms and Nacéra by the hand. Hamid, who was still asleep, stayed with my mother.

When I got home, I knocked.

No one.

I insisted again. An unknown woman opened the door.

- What is it?

- But... This is my home, here," I exclaimed, dumbfounded.

- Ah, no. This is my place. Who are you?

- I'm Faïçal's wife.

- Faïçal sold us the house. Where were you then?

- But when did you buy it?" I asked, more and more stunned.

- We paid and signed the deed yesterday.

- Furniture, clothes?

- There's nothing left in this house that belongs to you. Not even a sock, my good woman. He emptied it all yesterday.

Distraught, I returned to my mother's house. She was making coffee. It was still very early. My son and my brother Youssef were still asleep. I told her the terrible story I'd just heard. She cried out:

- How could he do that, but how could he?! Kick his wife and kids out?! How is that possible? Trust the men!

- Ma, take it easy. There's no need to wake them. Can you look after Hassina for me? I'll see if I can find him in the neighborhood where he works.

I had three small children. Hassina was still bottle-fed and I didn't even have enough money to buy her diapers. My brother, whom I still didn't speak to, would never agree to let us stay with my mother again. Where would I go if I couldn't find Faïçal?

On the street where he worked, I recognized some guys who knew him.

- You haven't seen Faïçal, have you?

One of them took me aside. He confirmed that the house had indeed been sold. He added:

- We saw him empty it. Your furniture is with a cousin of his. Down the rue de la Lyre.

I showed up at the cousin's house.

- Listen," I tried to negotiate, "I don't care about the furniture. I wouldn't even have a place to put it. I'd just like to get some clothes for the kids and myself.

- I can't give you anything. Take it up with your husband.

I left, dragging Nacéra by the hand. My daughter understood that something serious was going on. I tried not to panic her too much, but I was really shaken up myself. I walked for a long time, then sat down on the edge of a sidewalk to think.

I couldn't possibly stay with my mother. It would have created problems with my brother. So I went back, just to get Hassina, and took refuge at my uncle's place. I had to walk about ten kilometers with the girls, as I didn't have a penny in my pocket for transport.

- We told you not to marry her," my uncle said by way of consolation.

He couldn't put me up for too long either. Even though I really felt sorry for him, he had a large family and was already barely able to take care of them. I didn't want to be another burden.

So I went to visit a friend, Amira, whom I had supported a lot at a time when her children were young and her father had left.

- What exactly do you want?" she asked.

- Divorce. I don't want to be afraid of him or his reactions anymore. I want to move on. I want a home for my children.

- Then I'll help you divorce. I know someone who knows someone who works at the courthouse in Sénia. We'll go there.

- You have no proof of what you're saying," the judge told me. If you ask for a divorce, you won't be entitled to the house.

- But I'm telling you, I don't have a home anymore. I'm homeless. When things aren't going well in a couple and a woman doesn't divorce, it's so that her children can keep a roof over their heads. But we no longer have a roof over our heads. I can't even find him to explain myself to him. I want a divorce.

Despite the laws of the Family Code, which were not at all to women's advantage, the judges were understanding and, in 1995, I was able to get a divorce.

Like Hamid, I was entitled to a pension. Like Hamid, I never saw any of it.

10. Another Life

I had to get a job. I canvassed all the schools and administrations in Oran, Aïn Beïda and Sénia, applying each time as a cleaning lady. To no avail. Sometimes, I was simply told that there were no vacancies. More often than not, however, I was forced to accept a "droit de cuissage" in exchange for a job. This shocked me: I felt dirty and full of rage. These men aren't men, I thought. They're beasts. They sniff out misery like wolves sniff out blood. But I was also desperate: what would become of me and my children?

I carried them from house to house. From uncle to uncle. I tried to be as unobtrusive as possible, but with three children, it was difficult.

In the morning, I dropped Hamid off at school; my daughters I either left with family members or took with me. They would wait for me outside when I went in for an interview.

I'd never been out so much in my life. I'd never walked the streets so much. I walked with a quick step, haunted by the anguish of not being able to provide for my children. I walked with a quick step, so that no man in the street would think it possible to approach me.

As well as looking for a job, I was looking for a place to live. They were asking me for diplomas and tons of papers that I didn't have. I applied to the Opgi for social housing[3]. But nobody believed in it unless they had a very good piston.

As I passed a shantytown, I decided to take a closer look at how people lived there. I wandered into the little alleys that had been built haphazardly. It was dirty, it stank. But these people had a roof over their heads.

I stopped at the level of a corpulent woman with a dull complexion, sitting at the door of her gourbi.

- How do you get here?

- What do you mean by that?

- If I want to set up shop, do I have to ask someone for permission?

- If you want to settle down, you don't ask anyone. You build and that's it.

As I pondered this possibility, she invited me to drink a coffee that tasted like chickpeas, reserved for

---

3. Office de promotion et de gestion immobilière.

the poor. She asked me lots of questions. I explained my situation.

- I won't hide the fact that the area is risky for a single woman with small children. But if you have no choice... I live with my husband and children. You look honest to me. Put your hovel up next to ours. Maybe it'll discourage the bad seed.

That's how I met Khéra. She too looked honest to me, with her beautiful, frank smile.

With the help of my uncles, who nonetheless tried to dissuade me, and my new neighbors, we set up my makeshift gourbi: half-rusted sheet metal, reclaimed wood and plastic.

In this ramshackle house, with no water or electricity, where the window and door wouldn't close, clutching my little ones, unable to sleep a wink because I was so scared, I didn't have the courage to spend more than one night.

I then organized myself differently. During the day, when I wasn't running to the authorities, I stayed in the shantytown so as not to be a burden on my family. At night, however, I would take refuge with my children and my family.

Khéra, who had become my good friend, had told me that by living in this shantytown, you earned points with the Opgi. By resisting here, I might be able to get a real roof over my head sooner.

It was she who told me about Hassi Messaoud in 1996.

Algeria's richest city.

Money and work for everyone.

- There are a lot of foreigners, but it's often the Algerians who recruit for them. They take a good part of your salary. But after that, you still have enough to live on. In any case, much more than when you're a lorry driver like my husband is at the moment. Especially since he's on a fixed-term contract and will soon be out of work. So Hassi could be good. You just have to put up with the climate. Would you like to give it a try?

- Yes!

I answered without thinking for a minute. I felt I'd already considered all the other possibilities.

We told ourselves that, if we managed to keep some moncy aside, we could, a little later, buy our own houses and, maybe even, if we worked hard, set up a small business to survive.

Our dreams gave me courage.

I knew Hassi Messaoud from the 8 o'clock weather forecast on TV. It was the hottest place in the country, sometimes reaching 50°C! How could the Saharans survive such a climate? How could they stand Ramadan?

Later, I discovered that the true temperature of the region wasn't even announced, for fear that the people working there would flee; not to mention the workers from the North who went home for the vacations and, faced with the weather, decided not to return to their posts.

Hassi Messaoud is not the place you'd dream of staying to have a good time.

I had to convince my mother. No matter how many times I told her I couldn't find a job, no matter how miserable my situation was, for her it was out of the question:

- People will talk. People will speak ill of us and smear us. The shame will be on us again. If you leave, I won't talk to you.

- Ma, the shame is on me because I can't feed my children or house them! We sleep around. I see you on the sly with Youssef, who barely tolerates my children in your home. Do you think it's a good life? At least in Hassi, I might have a good salary. In five years, in ten years, I could buy a house and finally get my three kids together! I argued again and again until she gave in.

I sold the gold belt she'd given me for my wedding. It cost 50 or 60,000 dinars. I thought I'd leave her some money so she could look after my daughters while I settled in. But she refused to take them in. She was too afraid of Youssef. So I decided to take them with me.

I called Hamid's dad. I got in touch with his third wife.

- Is Mourad in?
- No, it's not. What do you want with him?
- I want to give him his son," I replied.
Silence.
- I'll pass it on.
I told Hamid that he would be staying with his father for a while:
- You see, we don't have a home. Sleeping in each other's houses isn't much of a life for a kid your age. I have to go to work to earn enough money to build a nice house for all of us.
It was a terrible blow. How else could she do it?
No matter how many explanations I flooded him with, none persuaded him; for his part, he was full of ideas to force me to stay with him. He wanted us to move in with his grandmother and beg Youssef to accept us. Or that I remarry his father: after all, my own father had been a polygamist and it hadn't killed anyone. Or we could live in the tin shack for good, which he thought was just fine. And what was wrong with living in a shantytown?
- The slum is dangerous for a single woman with children, full of cockroaches and rats, covered in filth

that won't leave us healthy for long. So much so that we too will end up looking like cockroaches.

- Cockroaches with a mommy," he mumbled sadly.

I took him in my arms:

- I must find work, my son, to feed you.

- But I can work! I'll sell chickpeas at the mimosa market and retail cigarettes in Moorish cafés.

His arguments, though they couldn't hold me back, touched me deeply.

If he'd known how much I didn't want to part with him, I wouldn't either!

- You have to go to school to keep learning things, to have a good job later on. You won't be staying with your father forever. It's just for the time being.

His father had asked me to hand over custody permanently if I wanted him to take care of her.

I agreed, with a heavy heart.

I couldn't tell Hamid.

I bought him his trousseau for the new school year, clothes and little gifts to cheer him up. I accompanied him to Mourad's house. He was sick for two days, having asthma attacks and sobbing uncontrollably. He refused to let me go.

I promised to take her to her new school before I left.

In front of the school gates, he cried over and over again, hiccupping that he didn't want to stay with his father or in that school, that he wanted to go home with me. His little hands clutched my body, and he couldn't let go.

I tore myself away from his pleading embrace and left without looking back. Almost running away. I could hear her screaming. Heartbroken. I cursed my life and the day I was born.

A final ordeal awaited me: I had to go to court to sign the paper transferring custody to Mourad. It was the only day of the week when such documents were drawn up.

I waited there for two hours. Then an official informed us that the prosecutor would not be coming.

It was the sort of thing that often happened. This contempt, this permanent lack of respect for citizens, made me get out of my depth and rage against the administrations. But that day, I refrained from commenting.

I rushed to my ex-husband's house to explain the situation. That I couldn't wait another week: Khéra and her husband were getting impatient.

He agreed to postpone this step until my next visit.

Relieved not to have had to sign that paper, I thanked God and my recently deceased paternal grandfather.

Certain that he was watching over us.

11. El Haïcha, the Filthy Beast

Khéra and her husband Mohamed were originally from Oued Souf, on the road to Hassi Messaoud. So we made a short stopover with their family.

In the morning, in the courtyard, I discovered the sand of the Sahara for the first time.

- And if we sweep up some of this sand, will we find stone or earth?

- If we sweep away some of this sand, we'll find sand," Mohamed replied. They both laughed a lot.

- It's obvious you're not from the South," Khéra gently mocked.

Mohamed had requested passes for us, without which we couldn't get into Hassi Messaoud. It was a bit complicated, but he had several maternal uncles working on the bases. We were waiting for their green light.

We arrived around Hassi at night. Mohamed's maternal uncle, who was a school principal, was waiting for us at the Haoud El Hamra dam[4]. He put us up in his house on the boulevards. In other words, on the residential roads.

When day broke, the light was so strong that it woke us up very early despite the fatigue of the long journey.

Outside, the tarmac road was surrounded by sand. The heat was already overwhelming. The sand was as black as coal. The houses, black too. It was explained to me that this was because of the large flares burning around the town.

There was a huge crowd. But where were all these people going? The men wore thick[5] *kachabias* and *chèches* around their heads.

- Are they beggars?" asked Khéra's son.

- No, they're the living dead," I replied, laughing.

But, in truth, I was terribly worried. How were we going to survive this climate? Would some die? How many would? Wouldn't it be dangerous for my daughters, who weren't used to this heat?

Rents, and life in general, were notoriously high in Hassi. So, before we arrived, Mohamed's uncle had found us a house in a "popular district", Bouamama.

---

4. Gendarmerie checkpoint located thirty kilometers from Hassi Messaoud, where passes are issued or checked, without which it is impossible to enter the town.

5. Long wool tunic.

11. El Haïcha, the Filthy Beast

To reach our new home, we had to leave the tarmac road, walk down a path covered with dirty sand, decaying plastic bags and other garbage, and enter equally filthy alleyways, made up of hundreds, if not thousands, of random buildings stuck together, and when this wasn't the case, the smallest space between them was invaded by garbage of all kinds.

My heart sank as we went deeper and deeper into this area that nobody, I later discovered, called Bouamama.

El Haïcha, "the filthy beast", is what everyone called this neighborhood.

Or rather, this huge shantytown in the middle of Hassi Messaoud. Ugliness and misery as far as the eye can see. Makeshift walls stretched for kilometers, hard-built but hastily erected. The gray of the cement, never covered by anything, brought us back to the misfortune and destitution of the people.

There were also garages that served as lodgings, rented out for fortunes to Algerians from the forty-eight *wilayas*[6] in search of work, by the owners, most of whom were neighbors.

My disappointment was immense.

Our accommodation was a tiny shack with two rooms, a narrow kitchen and a *haouch*[7], overgrown

---

6. The equivalent of the French prefectures. Administrative divisions on which *daïras* (sub-prefectures) and APCs (communes) depend.

7. Inner courtyard.

with sand, in which we washed with a small basin. The front door was only closed with a wire. Water, when it was available, was undrinkable. Electrical connections were dodgy, with wires hanging down, pulled out and connected to the owners' installations.

All this for an astronomical rent...

- It's just for the time being," Khéra reassured me, perhaps to convince herself that this situation would only be temporary.

She added:

- We mustn't forget why we're here.

I had to find a job fast.

Mohamed's uncles explained the situation to me and directed me to the subcontractors who were in charge of recruiting labor for the foreign companies.

I began my investigations early the next morning.

But after three or four days, I was taken over by a huge, nauseating depression. I'd just abandoned my son, sold my gold, travelled eight hundred kilometers by bus and rotten cab, only to discover that the hungry wolves hadn't spared this part of Algeria either. The droit de cuissage was the law here too.

- I have a vacancy. I can take your file. But do you want to go out with me?

What they were imposing on me there, I hadn't accepted in Oran, at 20°C on the water's edge, under the light sea breeze that caressed my face; and these

11. El Haïcha, the Filthy Beast

sub-humans imagined that I was going to give in at 60°C, with the sand sticking to your skin and that Satanic sun that wears you out with the slightest step? I felt a boundless hatred for these guys.

Under my tin roof in El Haïcha, I lay down all day long. I didn't want to think anymore. But it was impossible to let go. How was I going to feed my daughters if here, as in Oran, you had to sell yourself for honest work? I believe in and respect God. I say my five prayers a day. I didn't take off my *hijab* after my divorce for fear of a curse. And yet there was nothing positive in store for me and my family. No way out.

- Don't resign yourself. God is great," Khéra consoled me when she got home. I tell everyone I meet about you. We'll see. Maybe we'll get some good news.

I had 30,000 dinars left[8]. I decided to keep 2,000 aside and return to Oran as soon as the rest of my nest egg ran out. Come what may. But the last thing I wanted was to be a burden on my friends.

I only got up to look after the children, cook or do a bit of housework. The rest of the time, I just lay there. Wiped out by heat and despair.

One noon a month after our arrival, just as the children were finishing their lunch and I was doing the

---

8. 100 DA = 1 euro.

few dishes we had, there was a knock at the door. On the threshold, a woman with a ponytail. She asked me:

- Are you the Oranaise that Khéra brought back with her?

- Yes," I replied.

- Is Khéra there?

- She's asleep in the next room. I'll call her.

Khéra introduced me to Nadia, also from Oued Souf.

- Khéra told me about you. She told me you were a good cook. There might be a job for you in a company I know. They're legit. I'll give them your file today and you'll have to go and see them tomorrow morning. Can you do that?

This woman, in jeans, sneakers and sunglasses, who came in a white two-door Golf to our hovel, was an angel sent by God.

- God is great," I kept telling myself. He never let me go.

12. My First Job

The next day, at 6 a.m., I was at the company. We got an early start because of the weather, which even the air-conditioning units in the big SMEs couldn't keep down.

It was a *catering* company working for Toyota. My superiors explained my duties and told me my salary: 12,000 dinars. It wasn't very high for the region, but it suited me. They introduced me to the other members of the team. All women, from the four corners of Algeria, looking for work. To ensure their survival and that of their families, but also to protect themselves from terrorism, which was in full swing at the time.

I'd wanted the job so much that when I was offered the chance to start on the same day, I gladly accepted.

For the first time since Faïçal had sold the house, I had the feeling that doors were opening: at last, I could see a way out.

But my good mood soon gave way to other concerns. Khéra would soon be starting work too, and I couldn't find anyone trustworthy enough to look after my daughters: I didn't know the neighbors, and I didn't like our neighborhood.

So I phoned Baya, my older sister, to ask for help:

- Take Hassina and Nacéra for a year while I get things organized. I'll send you a monthly allowance, so you won't have to pay anything for them.

She refused:

- Nobody works here but me. How do you expect me to look after your girls? Life is hard for everyone. And she added, after a little hesitant silence: don't you want to take Widad with you and find her a little job until she passes her A-levels again?

I wanted to entrust my daughters to her, but I found myself waiting for my niece to arrive.

The heat was unbearable. On the street, I felt like I was walking with a giant dryer chasing me. I suffocated. I passed out. I was then taken to the emergency room, where I was given the traditional infusion of serum and other recommendations - drink lots of water, never expose yourself to the sun - reserved for "Tell people", as they called them. In other words, non-Saharans.

- It's your baptism, you're adapting to the south winds," Khéra said to tease me.

She and her whole family didn't have these problems.

A fortnight after my first job, I was offered a second. Again for the Japanese. Night work this time. Two hours of housework within the company, from 8pm to 10pm, for a salary of 9,000 dinars. I couldn't believe how much it paid.

Nevertheless, I asked for a week's delay, because how could I do this for my daughters? I was already anxious with only one job, but I couldn't refuse this new opportunity. It would give me quicker access to my two obsessions that kept swirling around in my head like flashing lights: house, project. House, project.

Back home with Khéra at the end of the day, still preoccupied, the smell of blood in the warmth of the clinker suddenly turned my heart upside down.

My little Hassina was lying under some blankets, a red-stained bandage on her face. Nacéra, distraught, told me that while playing outside, her sister had tripped and her face had been injured on a rusty tin can. Khéra's neighbors and cousins tried to calm me down. But I screamed:
- Why wasn't she taken to hospital?
- It's not part of Sufi tradition," I was told.
I was going crazy.
I called my sister back:

- Please take care of my daughters or ask Ma to do me this favor. Nacéra doesn't go to school because it's too far away. Hassina fell when I wasn't there, and they didn't even take her to hospital.

- I've already talked to her about it. She says she can't take them as long as Youssef is paying for the house. He'll never agree to having them around.

- Please try again. She won't have to pay a thing.

- On one condition, then: try to find work for my husband and two children. I can't stand being the only one to toil.

- I'll do everything I can, but I can't promise you anything.

My mother agreed to take in my daughters. Nacéra was able to go to school. Hassina was still too young. I agreed to work the night shift. I sent 10,000 dinars a month to Ma, as well as foodstuffs (coffee, sugar, flour, etc.) which were distributed to the employees when they approached the expiration date. I entrusted the products to the driver of the bus that made the Hassi-Oran shuttle; my mother would wait for him at the bus station to collect the precious parcels.

My niece, who had recently moved in with me, was having great difficulty acclimatizing and spent more time in hospital than at home. I found her a job, but it paid very little. Once the subcontractors had been paid off, he was left with a salary of just 7,000 dinars.

12. My First Job

- I'd rather put up with my brother's tyranny and my mother's bad temper than this climate of *djahanem*[9], she told me before leaving.

From then on, I went to work feeling serene and in good spirits. The atmosphere was friendly. Men and women did their chores side by side, and we teased each other and laughed a lot. Far away from our homes and families, we quickly became close-knit and fraternal. At the end of the day, we parted reluctantly. Before going to my second job, I liked to joke with the local children. I'd kiss the little ones over and over again. I tickled them. I loved having them by my side.

- What's the matter with you and these kids?" Khéra wondered when she heard us heckling happily.

- They remind me so much of my own. I feel like I'm with them.

---

9. Hell.

13. Hamid's Elopement

My son has run away.

My superior gave me seven days' leave.

I landed in Oran in a panic. For ten days, I wandered the region. I searched for him day and night, traveling the Oranie region like a madwoman: Aïn Beïda, Sénia, Sidi Bel Abbès - where his father lived. I was afraid he'd drowned in a small artificial lake there, so I searched every nook and cranny, examined every bush. I'd stand staring into the water for hours, convinced that his putrefied body would resurface before my very eyes.

Then I went to the courthouse.

His father said to me:

- Since you still have custody, it's up to you to take care of the paperwork.

I put out every wanted poster I could find. In newspapers, in police stations. I went down to the central police station in Algiers to ask them to put out a nationwide APB.

I had forgotten my son. I didn't understand how it was possible.

I hadn't called him for a year, for fear of his reaction. He had cried so much, coughed so much because of his asthma attacks triggered by tears! In the early days, not giving him any news tortured me. Whenever I saw a child his age, or something that reminded me of him, it hurt. But then... Afterwards, I stopped thinking about him and that was that. Slowly, I forgot him. In this way, I anaesthetized the pain I felt at the memory of him.

Finally, I was told:
- Mrs. Salah, we received a telegram from Sidi Bel Abbès. We found an 11-year-old child named Hamid. However, his surname is not Bouafioun as on the notice you filed, but Salah, like you.

He had given his grandmother's address. It was my child, it was him. I felt my strength drain. I fell.

I asked his paternal uncle to pick him up at the Sidi Bel Abbès police station and wait for me at my mother's house.

Hamid burst into tears when I arrived. He was skinny. He hadn't grown. He was clutching the little plastic car I'd given him. He sobbed without taking a step towards me. Tightly clutching his toy.

I took him in my arms and hugged him tightly:

- Don't run away like that again, Hamid!

- But you didn't call me. You told me you were going to call me and you didn't.

That night, he slept in my arms.

- I want to live with you, Ma. I miss Nacéra and Hassina too.

- You'll live with me, I promise. We'll all live together again. But not right away. Give me time to get organized. I've got to keep working to buy us a house. In the meantime, tomorrow I'll go back to Hassi, and you to your father. But I'll be back for you. I swear on the Koran. Sleep now, my beloved son. And don't worry about a thing. Everything will work out in the end.

The next morning, I took him back to his dad's house. I'd bought him a nice bicycle, which gave him back his beautiful smile for a few minutes, but triggered Mourad's anger, who knows why.

Being away from my son made me sick.

14. *Bigtel, Babaa, El Mairikaine*

Three months later, at Ramadan time, I asked for time off to be with my children. It wasn't granted.

I went anyway. I was desperate to spend Eid with them. I wanted to give them gifts, as is the custom. Smell them. To kiss them.

Nevertheless, I decided not to go and see Hamid. If he started crying or decided to run away after my visit, his father wouldn't forgive me.

I arrived at the home of Ahmed, my maternal uncle, on the eve of Eid. My mother was waiting for me outside, in the pouring rain, with my two daughters. I showered them with kisses. What a joy to finally feel them against me!

We all went shopping together, because I wanted to spoil them. My mother and sisters were not to be outdone. The next day, I spent the morning with them. Then I took the bus back to Hassi.

Not a store open on the road. A real desert for a thousand kilometers: a thirty-first day of Ramadan, in short.

I'd finally seen my daughters, but I'd lost my job.

A former colleague, Ourdia la Kabyle, visited me to tell me that Bigtel was recruiting.

What a dream it is to work for this company! Unlike other foreign bases, this American base, reputed to be the largest in Hassi Messaoud, never used subcontractors to recruit its employees. As a result, salaries were very good. But it was also without hope:

- Bigtel, they're too big for me. I don't have a piston. I don't play in the same league.

- Try your luck anyway. With God's help, you never know.

So I took his advice, and the next morning, very early, I took a cab to Bigtel. In front of the guardhouse, a security guard.

- Who sent you?" he asked.

- I'm nobody. I'll take my chances, that's all.

- You don't have an invitation, you haven't taken a test, nobody sends you and you just turn up like this?

- Yes, just like that.

He seemed compassionate. He made a phone call. Ten minutes later, a driver picked me up and drove me to the base. Huge. I'd never seen anything like it. The further we drove, the more intimidated I felt. There were endless cottages.

14. Bigtel, Babaa, El Mairikaine

An Algerian recruitment manager met me.

- Who recommends you?

- Someone very tall.

- Do I know him?

- I think everyone knows him," I said with a smile.

- But who is it?

- God! Who else could it be? I don't know anyone. I came with God's help, and that's all!

He laughed and put down his pen.

- What did you do before?

I hurriedly handed him my little file with my only certificate of employment. He seemed interested in my experience in the kitchen.

I had to carry out tests to make sure I knew how all the machines worked. Not just in the kitchen, but also in the laundry room, as I could be called upon to replace my colleagues. Everyone had to be versatile," he asserts. The truth is, an oven is still an oven, and a washing machine is still a washing machine. But it still impressed me.

After two hours, he pulled out a contract and explained that I would sign it the next morning, after the medical.

The infrastructure of their clinic was particularly impressive. The nurses and doctors were all Americans. Blood tests, lung x-rays, urinalysis, eye check-ups - they examined me from every angle. The medical questionnaire went on and on.

Finally, I held my contract in my hands and saw that my salary was double that of my old one. I was given two badges. One was for access to the base. Employees had to leave it at the entrance. The other indicated our blood type; we were not to part with it under any circumstances.

On weekdays, Bigtel was swarming with people.

As I worked in the kitchen, I had to take two showers a day. The first in the morning, the second at 1:30 p.m., before the next shift. These were particularly pleasant moments, which I savored to the full.

The company had a large gym, which I began to frequent assiduously at lunchtime. With my Walkman on, I worked out to the rhythm of the Oranian *chioukhas*, precursors of *raï*, or texts from the Koran.

We also had a fifteen-minute break, during which we drank coffee and nibbled delicious little cookies the likes of which I'd never eaten before. We were so fond of them that the camp leader doubled the order.

One day, there was a short-circuit which caused a huge fire with considerable damage in the kitchen. The cold room and pantry had caught fire. Fortunately, no one was around at the time. When we arrived, employees were clearing away the charred remains. Everything was burnt. Everything but the pork. For us Algerians, there wasn't even a little mutton left. Except... one of those famous cookie tins!

While we were laughing at her, an Algerian colleague from the administration, who had joined us to see the damage and who could read English, told us that these succulent little cookies were made from pork fat.

And so we learned that we had been in sin for almost a year of intensive snacking!

It wasn't our fault, as we couldn't read English or French, so we didn't know what was in it. On the other hand, we were very disappointed at the idea of not being able to eat any more.

We were amazed at how quickly the work was completed and the kitchens restored. Both admiring and mocking, we kept repeating among ourselves *"Bababa, El Mairikaine!* Bababa, the Americans!"

15. Family Reunification and Friendships

Khéra's husband Mohamed told me he'd found a job for my mechanic brother-in-law. He would be paid a good salary, given his qualifications and years of experience. He would be housed at the oil base where he would be working.

When I passed on the news to my sister, she announced that she would be sending her two children with him, so that they too could look for work. With winter coming, she told me, Widad would be able to cope better with the climate.

She told me that my cousin Lalia, who was in urgent need of work, also wanted to try the Hassi experience.

I couldn't possibly put all these people up with Khéra, who was about to give birth to her fourth child. I myself, occupying a whole room in the little shack, was beginning to feel like too much. So I decided to rent another house. I found a much larger one just two blocks from Khéra's. It was a stroke of luck. I didn't want to move away from my friend, whom I considered a real sister.

The rooms in this new apartment soon filled up: two of my colleagues, Assia and Wassila, who were also from the west of France and with whom I'd made friends, were complaining about being very badly housed, at an absurd rent. So I offered to let them live with us, for a small fee.

A little later, Lalia's niece, Nacéra, joined us, swelling the ranks of expectation and hope for a job that would improve our financial situation.

My brother-in-law Miloud, who got on rather well with the bottle, was sometimes too tired to return to his base after a good meal shared all together. So he preferred to sleep at home.

Our neighbors, who owned our house, taught him how to make the local alcohol, made from melon and wheat. Much cheaper than export spirits, and much more effective, they claimed, because it was much stronger. Although he enjoyed making it himself, Miloud found that there was nothing like a good Cuvée du Président, and often found himself running dry at the end of the month. No offense intended. I had great affection for this man, who behaved like a real father to me and my other sisters.

I was more bothered, however, by the actions of his son, my nephew, who was a real hothead. Frequently, a neighbor would come and tell me about a brawl he'd started. People thought he was my son. I prayed that my little Hamid would never be like him. He behaved badly towards his sister: sometimes he would come home in the early hours of the morning and wake her up to force her to make him something to eat. If she refused, he'd bawl her out. I raised my voice higher than he did. At that point, I could still hold it together a little.

Amar, my paternal cousin, also joined us. He lived on the base with Miloud, who had managed to find him a job, but, like my brother-in-law, most of the time he had dinner or spent his day off with us. We rediscovered the atmosphere of yesteryear: celebrations were real celebrations - whether for Eid, Mouloud or birthdays; Khera and all her little family joined us, and we shared real moments of joy. This community life was a real treat for us.

But not everyone was happy about our cohabitation. The locals began to gossip, finding the mix suspicious and out of place.

It was a neighbor we liked who informed us that a complaint had been lodged against us for bad morals and that a neighborhood investigation was underway. I was devastated. Every time you want to harm

15. Family Reunification and Friendships

someone, you accuse them of bad morals. Irritated, or rather mad with rage, I took all our papers and went to the police station.

On the spot, I drew up our entire family tree, complete with identity papers and family records. I explained that it would be better for Assia and Wassila to live with us as a family than to find themselves isolated and exposed to the lustful glances of men who harassed them with degrading and humiliating phrases every time they walked through El Haïcha or any other part of Hassi; like all women, in fact, who had the misfortune to walk alone. But nobody cared about that!

Embarrassed by the whole affair, they assured me not to worry: they would quickly conclude this investigation, which had been demanded by malicious tongues, jealous and envious of the family's good relations.

With the women, life was very well organized. Whether at home or at work, we were very supportive of each other: when one of us went on leave, the others would ask her to run a few errands, deliver money, collect administrative papers or mail from our families. If she had a second job, we replaced her while she was away.

Not to mention the new friends we've made outside work.

Starting with Fatéma, whom Khéra had introduced to me. Originally from Oued Souf, she too had lived in Hassi since childhood, sharing her home with her five daughters and six sons, all married and bigamists. We didn't even try to count her grandchildren!

It was the way she dressed that first caught my attention: sometimes dressed like a man, with her tergal pants and jackets; sometimes like a gypsy, or even a Peruvian, with her long brightly-colored skirts over her pants, and her felt hat, very rare in this region, over her scarf. She had a store that was a veritable shambles, where she bought and sold all sorts of things. She amused me greatly.

We quickly became close. Even though she lived on the other side of town, we often visited each other. In fact, as a rule, we were often at each other's houses. Friendship was very important in Hassi: most of us suffered greatly from distance and lack. Our get-togethers and solidarity were our remedy against the distress that threatened to make the weakest among us lose their heads.

Zahra, now known simply as Zaza, was one of these vulnerable women. She worked at 24[10] with Amar.

My cousin had taken a liking to her: her story had touched him deeply.

Her daughter had been taken away from her. So she started looking for her everywhere. I don't know whether it was then or when she came to live in Hassi

10. Sonatrach drilling base.

15. Family Reunification and Friendships

that she lost her footing a little. But she wasn't at the bottom of the abyss: she managed to live, work and share a room with other women. But she was often out of step. Sometimes, she stopped speaking.

She came to see me from time to time. She'd arrive with her canvas and embroidery materials, set to work and sigh. Sometimes she'd talk about her little girl as if she'd never lost her. Or, on the contrary, she would recall her disappearance. It was painful to listen to her. But more often than not, we shared long moments of silence, which she imposed on me and which I respected. I liked her. She was undergoing psychiatric treatment, but refused to buy her medication on her own. She would call on me to accompany her to the pharmacy.

In the mornings, around 4:30, I'd bump into her at the bakery. I wanted to pay for her cake. Despite her meager salary, she would never accept. She was very proud.

Between 1998 and 2000, my cousin helped her look for her daughter, to no avail.

16. Fatiha

M'barka, a colleague of Bigtel's, invited me to her son's circumcision.

- I'm renting a studio to Fatiha, a Western girl like you. It'll be a good opportunity to meet her," she told me.

She lived in the two-hundred-housing district next to our shantytown. A neighborhood that was said to be beautiful and had the ambition of being one of Hassi's future chic spots. For the time being, however, it was a huge construction site that progressed at the pace of heat-stunned men.

During the party, Fatiha was always busy, helping the M'barka girls serve coffee and cakes to the guests. It was a sign of good understanding between her and her owners. In fact, M'barka seemed to like her a lot. She told me that, when it got too hot, Fatiha would sleep in the *haouch* with her daughters to enjoy the coolness of the sand.

- She's like a daughter to me," she concluded.

- 8,000 dinars in rent for someone you consider your daughter is a bit steep, isn't it?" I retorted, trying to tease her a little.

She laughed yellow:

- I don't set the prices.

Fatiha was a slender, beautiful young woman of 25. Her matte complexion brought out the honey color of her eyes. Her face and arms were tanned, and I could tell from her slightly sunburned hair that she didn't wear a scarf outside.

When I didn't see her join us, I called her.

- Why don't you sit down so we can have a chat between women from the same country!

- You're the principal's girlfriend," she said in front of M'barka, her eyes laughing.

- You don't cover up outside.

- What's it to you? Are you the police or the FIS?" she replied, her eyes mischievous.

- I'm scared for you, that's all.

- Be afraid for yourself. I cover myself when I'm cold.

We laughed. Then we talked at length about his home town, Saïda. And my own, Oran, some fifty kilometers away.

She offered me a tour of her studio. I'd rarely seen anything like it in Hassi. There were lovely curtains on the windows and embroidered doilies everywhere.

The TV and fridge looked new. On one of the walls, painted white by her, she told me, was a poster of the snow-capped mountains of the Djurdjura.

Usually, people from Tell who come to fill our types of jobs pack as little personal belongings as possible. There was no room for the superficial in Hassi Messaoud. At least, not for people like us.

- Are you planning to settle here?

- And why not? Life is beautiful when I don't spend it with my head under the faucet so as not to die in the furnace.

- And why don't you rent this studio with a couple of other girls? It would cost you less.

- I'm like my father, I hate girls," she replied mischievously.

Later, when we became friends, she told me the reason for this joke.

As her mother carried her in her womb, she asked her husband what he would do if their child were a girl:

- I'd take my jacket and go," he declared.

The mother, who had already had eight children from her two previous husbands, had never been mistaken about the sex of her fetuses.

- It's going to be a girl," she announced. The father-to-be then grabbed his jacket and headed back to his first wife.

16. Fatiha

Fatiha was loved and pampered like a little princess: most of her brothers and sisters were already married.

When she learned, at the age of 16 or 17, that her father, contrary to what her mother had told her, was not dead, she wanted to know what he looked like.

Unfortunately, he didn't share this curiosity:
- You're here now, when all these years you've never even looked for me?" he said when he saw her.

At the time, Fatiha was passionately in love with a man who was madly in love with her. But her father refused to give his permission for the marriage. So she had to settle for a religious union.

She and her husband enjoyed four months of intense happiness. Before he was killed in a car accident. It was all down to bad luck, or the driver running the red light. Fatiha was pregnant. She was 19 years old.

She resisted despair for the child growing inside her. Eight months later, she gave birth to a beautiful little girl weighing 3.1 kilos. She nursed the tiny little being from the heart before going to sleep.

When she woke up, her baby was gone. She looked all over the hospital, asking questions, screaming and crying, but no one had seen anything. No sooner had the investigation been opened than it was closed. Was it to protect influential people or simply a lack of interest in a simple young woman of the people? She never found out. Her family and in-laws were upset by this new misfortune that had befallen them and Fatiha, against which they could not fight. The young woman plunged into deep distress, which only the years and the support of her mother, always at her side, were able to alleviate, without ever completely curing.

She arrived in Hassi on an afternoon in August 1999, the worst time of year to face the desert... But she had no choice: she had desperately looked for a job in Saïda, without success.

Her maternal cousin, already living in Hassi, had offered to take Fatiha in and help her find a job. She asked for 40,000 dinars to pay for the pass, travel and living expenses for the first month. Without question, the mother paid this astronomical sum. She also gave her daughter 10,000 dinars for incidental expenses.

Fatiha, stunned, discovered that the trip cost much less and the pass was free.

In Hassi, her cousin forbade her to go out, on the pretext that she was young and in danger of being lured away by the local men.

- I'll find you a job," she kept telling him.

If she wanted to call her mother, her cousin would do it for her.

She was sequestered.

After twenty-one days, she escaped through a window. Completely lost in the city, she wandered the streets until she came across a taxiphone where she was able to call her mother. In tears, she told her everything.

A man waiting a few steps away overheard the conversation and offered to help her. Now wary, she didn't answer him. But he followed her.

- Listen, I'm not going to hurt you, I'm married and I love my wife. I've got kids too. I just want to help you. If you're looking for a house, I can find you one you can sleep in tonight. If you're looking for a job, I can introduce you to a subcontractor. After that, we don't even have to see each other again, if you prefer.

The man was honest and kind. Thanks to him, she was able to get a roof over her head and a job. She never saw him again. She would have liked, though, to thank him. To thank him for helping her without demanding anything in return, while the men's frustration was immense.

His gratuitous gesture gave her renewed hope in humanity.

17. Hamid in Hassi

On one of my regular calls to Oran, my mother announced:

- I went to see your son at his father's a couple of days ago, and all he could do was cry. So I picked him up before you had to go and visit him in the loony bin. Don't worry, he's doing better.

At last, I could phone him quietly and hear from him regularly. But the situation over there was difficult. Youssef couldn't stand the presence of my children.

I called Baya. I asked her to send Hamid, with his school file in hand, by bus as soon as possible.

It was his first year at college. He had always done well at school despite his worries. He came to me, with his bike and without his file. My sister hadn't had time to take the necessary steps to get it back.

I was still able to enroll him in a secondary school not far from my friend Fatema's home. Her grandson, Hassan, went to the same school. They became fast friends. He rode his bicycle to school every morning. He often had lunch at Fatema's house. I felt he was happy.

Our friend soon urged me to move Hamid into her home, so that he could avoid the bike rides, the 4x4s and the hit-and-run drivers, and stay in Hassan's company. I accepted her proposal. I went to see him every day.

But her school file still hadn't arrived. The school gave me a month to sort it out. I asked my sister to get busy.

When she finally managed to collect it, I waited impatiently; but the bus driver to whom we all regularly entrusted our parcels for our families and delivered theirs for a small tip, had nothing for me. My sister had left the file at the bus station, with an agent we didn't know.

He was lost.

I called Hamid's old school.

- Madam, the day your sister came in, the photocopier was out of order. I told her to go and make a photocopy of the file and give me the original, but she refused. I couldn't force her.

How was I going to explain this to Hamid's college? The school agreed to extend my deadline by another month.

I called the Oran academy. Without a file, they couldn't do anything. The same goes for the Ouargla academy.

The month passed. Hamid hasn't been able to get back to school.

When I finally had time off, I went to the organizations I'd contacted. I couldn't understand why there was no solution. I couldn't accept that his fate was sealed because of a misplaced file. I told my story, I tried to convince, I begged each of my interlocutors.

Nothing to do.

My son wandered around, his soul in pain, while his classmates attended their lessons. He could see it made me sad.

- It doesn't matter," he consoled me. The most important thing is that we're together.

Fatema suggested I move in with her rather than take my son back to El Haïcha.

One of the rooms she rented became available.

The idea won me over immediately. I was getting tired of our family life: I was spending far too much money, I was paying half the rent for the house on my own, and my nephew had become infernal. What's more, I had no doubt that getting out of El Haïcha would do me a world of good. I invited Assia and Wassila to come with me, but they preferred to stay.

Very quickly, Fatéma refused the rent I paid her every month.

- This is your home. So make yourself at home.

When I came home late from work, she would save me my share of dinner. She was very friendly with my son. All her attentions, which I had never known before I met her, touched me deeply. I felt she was closer than a sister. She was my ally.

She wanted me to marry her eldest son for the third time, "to seal our bond". I didn't want to, because he was a real idiot.

I decided to stop working at night to take better care of Hamid. He had to adapt to the climate.

On sandy days, he would say to me:

- It makes you want to stop breathing.

I plugged our ears with absorbent cotton to protect them, and put a little in our nostrils as a filter.

When the heat was too much, we slept in the *haouch*. I taught him how to make his bed in the local fashion. He didn't like it at all. At first, I too found the method restrictive: flatten the sand with a straight wooden board so that not a single bump remained; hose it down for a long time; the sand, after absorbing the water at an impressive rate, would then start to release steam; when there was no more smoke, you had to hose it down again for a while. Finally, we could lie down on the ground in the cool. We covered ourselves with a sheet and plugged our ears. We could then hope to sleep for a few hours.

Every evening, when my day's work was done, I'd go home to do my ablutions and prayers, pick up a few things before joining friends on the base, in search of an air-conditioned room. If Hamid felt like it, he'd come with me. We didn't get home until 1 or 2 in the morning. While I got up between 4 and 4.30 a.m. for my prayer before getting ready and going to work, he slept as long as the temperature allowed.

Two buses took turns picking us up. On lucky days, we took advantage of the air-conditioned bus. I'd go back to sleep for three quarters of an hour or an hour, by the time it had picked up all my colleagues. When we boarded the other bus, I was swimming, sweating all the water out of my body during the journey.

It was when the days were particularly stifling that I dreamed most of my home in Oranie, where my children and I would finally be reunited.

I regularly pestered my uncle Ahmed to find me a plot of land. But when he found one, I hesitated: the neighborhood where it was located wasn't a dream, because it was full of *zawalis*, very poor people.

My mother convinced me to buy it:

- At least it's cheap. You'll be able to build quickly and have your children with you.

Cheap, cheap… 200,000 dinars all the same! It took the help of my friends, work colleagues and savings to finally buy it. Thanks to my mother, who no longer took my full pension, I was able to pay off my debts fairly quickly. But how to build the house?

I wasn't happy to hear about my daughters. As my brother couldn't stand them, Ma always managed to keep them out of his sight and hearing. If he came home unexpectedly, she would hide them in the kitchen cupboard and tell them not to make any noise. On weekends, in the scorching sunshine, rain or shine, she would take them out to eat and only return at the end of the day. It became urgent to put an end to this situation, which was unbearable for my mother and daughters.

My uncle Ahmed, a mason, saw me worried and impatient, and offered to start work on the house. For a check of 30,000 dinars, he bought all the necessary materials. When I finally got there, excited and happy, I found that the work had barely begun... There wasn't even a slab yet. And the money was already gone. I was terribly disappointed. At this rate, the house would never be ready for another five or ten years.

I made promises to my children that I couldn't keep.

I went round the family. This time, Khadidja advanced me some money. Once again, my colleagues and friends joined in.

- Build me a tin roof. Put me a front door with wire for a lock, I don't care. I'm used to it by now. The main thing is that it goes fast and I can quickly get my children together in the same house," I told my uncle.

I began to dream: in a few years' time, maybe Hamid could take a training course with Ahmed, who earned a good living.

I'll hire a woman to look after them when I'm in Hassi.

I'd give up households.

And I could take all my vacations off to spend them with them.

18. Signs

In 2001, Bigtel downsized. That didn't bother me. From then on, I had my bearings in the city: I was back in work within a week.

It was also a *catering* company, Algerian this time, but with a Western boss. Its mission was to manage all hotel services, including all catering, for the American base, Halliburton. Same type of tasks, then. But less well paid. Fortunately, there was a good atmosphere here too. And although I saved less money, I still managed to save for the site.

I had made friends with a young girl who had joined the company the same day as me. Halima. This very pretty girl was a Chaouia[11] from Khenchela[12] who swore and blasphemed like a boy when she got carried

---

11. Originally from the Aurès, a plateau in eastern Algeria.
12. City of the Aurès.

away. And she often did. Her fine features contrasted with her coarse language and made me laugh.

Her father and uncle worked as handymen on a remote base in the city where they were housed, while she shared a room with her sister Abida, which they rented from a lady in a slum in El Haïcha.

Her father, uncle and sister had to return home to Khenchela for a vacation that she was not entitled to, as she had just arrived. She begged me to move in with her for the duration of their stay in Khenchela. She was afraid to be alone.

I refused, but her father insisted, telling me again and again that he wouldn't rest easy for her, so I finally gave in. It's true that the atmosphere was becoming increasingly uncertain for single women.

In Algeria, but especially in Hassi, young women walking unaccompanied by a man were constantly harassed, often in a rude manner.

Not to mention the aggressiveness that was increasingly added to the humiliating behavior of these men. We were regularly insulted. The women's tactic was to ignore them, to avoid physical aggression.

But Halima couldn't keep her mouth shut. Her Aurès blood was boiling, and she was quick to react, spouting a string of insults even more vile than those spat in our faces. The men were stunned every time.

18. Signs

That's when I pulled her by the arm to get away before things got out of hand.

This masculine behavior became our daily lot whenever we stepped outside. Locked away in our barracks, we only ventured outside for the bare minimum: work, shopping, the taxiphone.

As for the rest, either we had a car or we did without.

One evening, as we had left work a little late and there was no more transport, we were given a lift by a colleague, on the recommendation of our camp leader. In front of the house, a group of young people were waiting; they insulted us when they saw us.

- Impure! Sluts!" shouted one.

- Cover yourself up, you whore, and stay at home instead of taking our jobs," another guy spat two centimeters from Halima's face, who wasn't wearing the *hijab*.

For the first time, she didn't react. They terrorized us with their hateful faces and barricading bodies. The colleague at the wheel of his car, against all odds, didn't move a muscle to defend us:

- Talk to them. If you calm them down, they might listen to you," Halima whispered, her voice trembling.

- Get out of the way, get out of the way," he said, timidly. Clearly, he didn't want to get involved and was in a hurry to turn back.

The owner came to our rescue. She quickly let us in before trying to reason with them.

Perhaps we should have paid more attention to this incident.

But it was the school vacations: my brother-in-law, my sister and I had rented a small house in Laayoune, a seaside resort a few kilometers from Oran, so that the children could enjoy the sea. I had already sent Hamid, who would soon be joined by his sisters. I was planning to spend two weeks with them myself during my August break. Men could insult me, but that was all that mattered to me: for the first time, I could offer my children a real vacation. And soon, I'd be sharing it with them. The idea made me euphoric.

On July 13, 2001, three to five hundred men passed on the message.

That evening, anything went!

Those who had never seen naked women would see; those who had never fornicated would fornicate.

- Allahou akbar! El Djihad fi sabil Allah! *God is great! Holy war in the name of God!*

The starting signal was given.

Crossing a cloud of dust raised by their determined steps, they threw flaming tires into the middle of the road to prevent anyone from coming to the women's aid.

In the distance, a man waved a gray shirt in his hand. He was calling to them.

Like hungry wolves, they pounced on their first victim.

19. Fatiha, the First Victim

It must have been 8 p.m. when Fatiha, who was dozing off watching TV, heard the hubbub of a crowd.

- Hassi Messaoud and its oil bases are the safest zone in Algeria. Terrorism will never get here," she mused, glancing at her doorstep.

Nacer, his baggage handler neighbor, also left his house. Concerned, he said:

- Fatiha, it looks like things are heating up. We don't know what's going on. Come and take refuge with us, it's safer.

This proposal tempted her, but she didn't think it was prudent. What if the police turned up at his house just then? Indeed, under the pretext of policing the morals of society, unmarried couples were taken in and brought to justice. A neighbor's denunciation was enough for the police to break into your home and take you away if they deemed you suspicious.

- Coming out handcuffed in front of the neighbors, what a humiliation! she thought.

She declined Nacer's offer.

She locked her door. She lay there again, in front of the television.

The day before, Fatiha had wanted to call her mother to announce her forthcoming arrival at the family home. In front of the taxiphone entrance, three hundred meters from her home, a man had insulted her.

Fatiha had taken fright.

Everything about him was frightening. His eyebrows wagging in all directions. His big hands gesticulating as he fulminated:

- Dirty Oranaise! Dirty whore!

Just as she was about to turn back, heart pounding, he grabbed her violently by the arm and slammed into her face.

A circle of onlookers had formed around them. Fatiha had expected nothing from them. She was well aware of the tacit agreement that when a woman is beaten up in the street, no man should intervene.

So she waited for the blows to stop raining down, then, bent double, went to the police station to lodge a complaint.

They weren't interested. She was a nuisance. No policeman had come to check whether the assailant was still holding the wall of the taxiphone. She had,

19. Fatiha, the First Victim

however, obtained a document certifying her statement.

She was ashamed to go to work with a black eye. The colleagues, the boss. The looks. No one would say anything. But they would think:

- It was a boyfriend who hit her.

That's for sure. So she'd like to explain. Attestation in support.

- We're all there. Obsessed with what people will say.

The next day, the camp leader sent him to the doctor, an Algerian. Gentle and considerate, he applied ointment around her eye to deflate the hematoma. He said a few comforting words and advised her to take the day off to rest. His kindness had soothed her.

She still wanted to phone her mother. From her home, she took a cab to the taxiphone. She paid him, asked him to wait for her.

To hear his mother's voice...

She didn't report the assault. She just told her he was coming the next day. The joy of her mother's laughter warmed her heart more surely than any balm! She could see his beautiful tattooed face, his mouth pierced by damaged teeth.

- I've saved some money, Ma. I'll take you to the dentist and he'll fix your teeth," she told him.

- What comes out of my mouth doesn't come back, my daughter. Seeing you will be my greatest joy.

She left the store, feeling light-headed and delighted.
Outside, no more cabs.
She didn't look at the men. She walked fast. Head down. Back bent.
Someone whispered to him:
- Tonight will be your night.
She didn't straighten up. She quickened her pace.

In her area, she was less afraid. Her neighborhood wasn't bad and her neighbors were mostly established families. Fifty meters to the right, the doctor, originally from Algiers. A bit moody, but not mean. Just beyond, the gendarme and his seven children. Opposite, a policeman who also had a large family.
She was a good neighbor to everyone, but got on particularly well with the young people from her region who worked at the airport as baggage handlers, including Nacer. They all lived together with him. They were kind and respectful. They helped each other whenever possible: she, by having their laundry done at her work's laundry room; they, by carrying water packs to her home.

The noise of the crowd was getting closer. Fatiha turned up the TV to hear better.
Just then, a man's voice shouted from his window:
- L'Algéroise is here! Come and see! L'Algéroise is here!

19. Fatiha, the First Victim

She jumped up, caught sight of a guy waving to the crowd in a gray shirt. Panic-stricken, she shakily closed the shutters, turned off the TV, and curled up in a ball in the corner of the studio, breathing hard.

All we could hear was the sound of the fan.

Then, loud banging on the door as we tried to break it down.

First on the shoulder. Then with iron bars. The door held. Now they were at the window.

- With the bars, they'll never get in, she thought, to reassure herself.

But the bars were ripped off in one go with the cinder block around them.

- I'll tell the owner that his bars are crap," she said to herself, both furious and trembling with fear.

A guy jumped into the dark room. He lit a lighter. He immediately spotted Fatiha, transfixed with fright. He grabbed her violently by the hair.

- Turn on the light.

- My brother, I don't know where the light is anymore," she managed to say in terror, sobs in her voice.

They groped for the switch. Fatiha had to press the switch.

- So, you dirty whore, you bitch, you're well installed!

- Brother, I live alone. You can see there's no one. What have I done to you? I've got my papers. Take what you want! Take everything! I've got my pay in the cupboard. Take my gold...

She was punched in the eye. Stunned, she fell to her knees.

At her feet.

He was wearing patched leather sandals, with string for straps.

He tore off her tank top with a knife. Other men were coming through the window. She implored God to help her.

He pulled her shorts and panties down to her knees. Outside, they were still trying to break down the door.

Every time she screamed, the men outside chanted:

- *Allahou akbar*, God is great!

Every time one guy hit her, she'd find herself in the clutches of another, who would in turn hit her and send her hurtling into the arms of the next tormentor. She staggered and tried to get up, but her feet got caught in her shorts, which had slipped down over her ankles.

Ten. Now there were ten.

And still she staggered, and still she tried to get up; while they continued to beat and manipulate her like a rag doll. She gave up her modesty, her shorts and panties, took them off herself, so she wouldn't lose her balance again.

Her gold chain was ripped off. And as her rings wouldn't slip from her fingers, they began to burn

19. Fatiha, the First Victim

her flesh. One of them pulled out a knife to cut her phalanges:

- Brother," she yelled, "you don't have to cut off my fingers! Spit on the rings, or pee on them, they'll slip off!

She felt his slimy, stinking spit on her burnt fingers.

When the door finally gave way, they threw her outside, naked as the day her mother gave birth to her.

- My God, save me!

But the infernal saraband continued.

Armed with iron bars, knives and clubs, she could no longer count her attackers. The circle became immense, she was alone and tiny at the center of their stares and their hatred.

Allahou akbar; and slaps, punches, kicks.

Allahou akbar; thrown skywards, it crashed to the ground.

Allahou akbar. They bit her on the lips. Dragged her across the floor by her ankles. They bit her on the breasts. Dragged her by the hair.

Allahou akbar. One of them melted a plastic bottle of mineral water with fire before sticking it on her back. She felt her flesh burn.

Allahou akbar.

And the youyous of the women.

There were clumps of hair on the floor. Her blood was on the floor.

All the neighbors were there. They didn't react.

She screamed through her tears:

- Nacer, my brother, help me!

Despite the blows he was receiving, he tried to squeeze through the attackers' legs to get closer to her.

- Fatiha! Don't scream! Don't scream! Play dead, Fatiha! Hold your breath. Play dead so they'll let you go!

But how can you play dead when your fingers are digging into your vagina?

A tall black man with a red bandana threw her over his shoulder and ran to the cemetery.

- Ma, Ma! Don't leave me!

The broken iron door was a real cleaver. He wanted to block her head against the wall and slam the door to guillotine her.

- Today, I'm going to slit your throat and that of your God!

She struggled, screaming. She begged him.

Other men joined her. They took her back. They took her home. Opposite the policeman's hut.

The policeman left his house. He remained on his doorstep, contemplating the spectacle.

The gendarme didn't come out.

Thrown to the ground, she felt a whole hand raping her, tearing at her insides. *Allahou akbar*! It was the big black man in the red bandana.

He withdrew his bloody hand and wiped it across his face.

- Here's your honor! Eat it, whore!

She looked at the man then looked away.

To die!

Through the blood and dust, she recognized Samir, the friendly young grocer from whom she had been shopping. What she thought was a heart-rending howl turned out to be a whisper, barely audible:

- Samir, little brother, save me..." she said, holding out her arm.

He took her hand. With the other, he stabbed her between the shoulder and the armpit.

She recognized the long red knife he used to cut butter.

Using sand and ripped-up paving slabs, they buried her up to her neck.

They kicked his head.

A police car returning from the airport, intrigued by the crowd, approached. The men fled.

- This one would have been better left there," said one policeman. He began to dig it up, while another called for reinforcements.

The men were coming back.

The police took her home to safety.

In his studio, there was nothing left. Everything, absolutely everything, had been emptied.

They had taped his criminal record to the wall, with an inscription above it: "This is all that will be left of your corpse."

A wire hung from the ceiling chandelier.

Maybe to hang her.

One of the policemen took off his jacket and covered her.

The assailants were getting too close. The police put Fatiha in the Land Rover. They drove off, firing into the air. The crowd dispersed.

- Ask Aziz to tell my mother that I love her and that she forgives me," Fatiha managed to say before closing her eyes.

The firefighters took her to the morgue, believing her to be dead.

Armed with clubs, sticks, knives or sabres, the men split into small groups of fifteen, thirty or sixty and dispersed throughout the town.

Night now enveloped them.

Exhilarated by their first victim, driven by the worst desires, they took to the streets, cut through the dunes and wove their web through every thoroughfare so that no woman would escape their grasp.
They were led by guides whose job it was to identify the culprits, and whose comings and goings they scrupulously monitored.
Illuminated by the braziers they had lit, they broke down the doors of the gourbis and garages that served as dwellings.

Many of them raped their wives, looted and ransacked their meager homes.

20. The Night of the Massacre

It must have been midnight. Halima, Widad and I were getting ready for bed.

As we pounded the sand, strange noises came to us from afar. At first, we didn't understand. Then, the words became more precise. A crowd was approaching, chanting: *Allahou akbar. El Djihad fi sabil Allah*!

- They wage war at midnight! exclaimed Halima, not quite convinced.

I opened the courtyard door. A cloud stretched for hundreds of meters: the gathering must have been dense to raise so much dust. Nevertheless, I could make out fifty or a hundred men massed at the entrances to nearby *haouchs*.

Women's screams tore through the night. I slammed the door in panic. I slipped on my *hijab* and *khimar*[13] at full speed as the women's screams and the men's

---

13. Scarf.

vociferations drew ever closer. Where to flee? There was no way out. We were surrounded. The owner managed to reach us:

- They'll be here soon. You have to hide, come on," she said.

- No, we have to get out of here," replied Halima, terrified, while Widad hesitated.

- You won't take three steps before they catch you," our landlady retorted.

- I'd rather give it a shot than sit back and wait.

- Halima, you are two young girls. They're going to inflict the worst torments on you. Lock yourselves in the small room! If you ever get out of this, go to 1800, to Fatema's house. If we never meet again, tell my children and my mother that I love them.

The landlady and I hid Halima and Widad in a sort of discreet storeroom at the back of her house. That's when we heard loud banging on the courtyard door. As if someone wanted to break it down. The same violent, disquieting noises echoed in the neighbors' homes.

- Hide in my house!" urged the landlady, pushing me into the corridor before quickly closing the door behind me.

Outside, men were bellowing at her:

- Bring out the women!

- There are no women here," she retorted in an authoritative voice.

- Don't lie. We saw them being dropped off in a Toyota. There were three of them. Get them out if you don't want us to go over your body too," they threatened as they forced their way into the *haouch*.

I opened the door. Three men stood in the middle of the courtyard. The third, the oldest, must have been in his fifties, and I knew him. I'd run into him from time to time. Mohamed E'chaoui. He was holding a small sheet of paper in his hand, a list, I think.

- Ah, there you are," he says. We've been looking for you.

- I didn't do anything. Leave us alone! We didn't do anything! For God's sake, leave me alone! I begged.

- Let yourself go and we'll tell the others outside that we couldn't find you.

- I can't believe it! I'd rather go out again! Please...

- Get out, you won't survive very long," said another, while the third shouted aggressively:

- Tell us where your girlfriends are.

Outside, close to the house, the men were chanting *Allahou akbar* over and over again!

- They went out. I don't know where they went," I declared, my throat dry.

- Liar! Come over here. Sleep with us and we'll spare you.

I rushed to the door; on the other side, braziers lit up the sky. Men were throwing clothes and papers into them. There were so many fires, you'd have thought it

20. The Night of the Massacre

was daylight. There were about fifty of them, blocking the road between our house and the neighbors. They started shouting and insulting me. One of them wore a red bandana around his forehead; he had a big dagger in his hand. Others had clubs and sticks.

They were all heading my way. Who to beg?

They promised me the worst insanities.

- It's in the name of God that you want to put me through all this," I screamed.

I felt a knife rip through my belly. Blood gushed out with a violence that surprised me. It was the man with the bandana who had struck; his blade was now red.

He threatened me in an angry voice:

- Tell us where the girls are, or we'll consume you, we'll cut you into pieces!

- This is not Islam! This is not Islam," I cried, haggard and shocked.

I pressed my hand against my wound. My finger penetrated the gaping wound.

A huge shock on my face. Everything turned red. Blood was pouring out.

Hands, lots of hands, tore off my clothes, scratched my breasts, my thighs, tried to tear them apart.

I fainted.

Half-conscious, I heard men shouting:

- Police! Police!

- I'm dreaming, I thought.

But the men suddenly moved away and a voice exclaimed:

- Look over there, it's Rahmouna!

I knew these policemen. They leaned over me. Then they disappeared from my field of vision. Again, the sky filled with smoke.

And the attackers reappeared.

- They're going to finish me off, I thought.

One of the policemen threw himself on top of me to protect me, and was stabbed in the back. I felt his blood spill over my body.

I was covered with a sheet. I was evacuated on the same stretcher as the policeman, there weren't enough.

I felt I was leaving. I struggled not to sink into the dark.

To see my children again. Just to see my children again.

21. The Hospital

I made it to the hospital. I was lifted off the stretcher.

Standing in the room, I saw all those women. I knew almost all of them. One of them was sobbing. The beds were all occupied.

I started to fall apart. I was caught. I was laid on a bed where a woman was already lying. It was Fatiha. Completely bloodied.

I was out of air. I was suffocating. Half-awake, I spotted a woman doctor. She inserted a tube down my throat, into my lungs. I was suffocating even more. She sucked. Blood. Sand. I started breathing again.

We were lying on the plastic mattress. Fatiha was covered with a blood-soaked sheet. Her face, a mass of puffy, purplish flesh, was unrecognizable. She didn't move.

- She's dead," I thought before slipping back into a comatose sleep, overcome by the sobs of the women around me.

I kept fainting and coming to. Suddenly, I felt someone shake me, and then I was hit in the face with a mouthful of water. I opened my eyes. It was Zaza. She had wrapped herself in a dirty, blood-stained sheet. She was clutching a small bottle of water. She was crying.

- Rahmouna, I feel sick. Go get me my pills. You know very well that if I don't take them, I won't feel well. They made me eat the whole dog bowl... I think my arm is broken. Rahmouna, I've got to take my pills," she implored, pulling me up by the arm.

- Don't pull me like that. I can't get up, Zaza. I'm sorry. I can't help you. I can't help you, I whispered before my heavy eyelids closed again.

One by one, we brought back women. Now there were some lying on the ground. Those who had the strength were crying. It was their despair and humiliation that their sobs evacuated, it was their courage and tenacity from years of living, working and waiting in Hassi Messaoud that their sobs carried away.

I was shaken again. It was a man in *kachabia*. No. It was Fatema, disguised as a man so she could cross the town unhindered. She lifted my sheet with a trembling hand, glanced around with concern, covered me up, her face decomposed. Then she turned to the wall and burst into tears.

At the end of the room, I saw Lalia, my niece, collapsing. I was helpless. She was lying in a terrifying red pool. A doctor shouted to a nurse:

- We've got to get him to the OR!

- Fatéma, lend me your phone, I want to call my children," I said in a breath. She was one of my few friends with a cell phone.

- Listen, Halima and Widad are safe and sound. They thought you were dead. They saw pools of blood by your door and your clothes in tatters. They came to my house. Your nephew Boualem was there. He called your family to warn them. I'm going to call them to reassure them. But you can't talk to them in this state.

I fainted again.

In the morning, in the light of day, we discovered the horror of our condition.

Faces swollen, deformed by haematomas. Bloody bodies. Open chairs. And the smell. Flies. The moans.

How many of us were there? Fifty? Sixty? I found out later that some of them had taken cabs right after their attack, without going through the hospital, to get back to their towns.

Taos, the Kabyle woman, was one of the least affected. I knew her by sight: she must have been 23, she lived with her parents and brothers. She was hit on the nose. As she was running away, a man on a motorcycle stopped to rescue her. Now she was the one helping the women who had started bleeding, because the violence had triggered their periods or injured their intimacy; she tore sheets into strips of cloth, which she then placed between our red, dripping thighs. I don't know why I was so touched by her gesture; it was as if, with these bits of cloth, she was giving us back a little bit of dignity by preventing us from spilling our blood like animals.

She shouted round and round:

- But nobody comes to help us ! But nobody comes to treat us !

That was the question for all of us: why weren't we being cared for anymore?

Using a bottle of mercurochrome she'd found somewhere, Taos herself cleaned and disinfected our wounds, which were still full of dirt. She came to each of us and helped us drink water from a mineral water cap: we hadn't had anything to drink since the day before.

Outside, we heard yodels. Yodels of joy. When we were nothing but wounds and blood. How could anyone so openly rejoice in our misfortune?

No one was allowed to visit us. Friends and colleagues were expelled. Nevertheless, some people managed to smuggle us food or see us, provided they greased the palms of the nurses and planters. Fatema managed to return with a *gandoura*[14], clogs and some food, which we gobbled up in a few minutes.

In the evening, they brought us a newspaper about us. It was the Arabic-language daily *El Khabar*. It presented us as prostitutes who had come from all over Algeria to work in brothels. It was the coup de grâce: with an article like that, we knew that public opinion would condemn us. What would our families think? We were devastated. Fatiha cried. She begged:

- Collect all the newspapers. Tell them they're not allowed to distribute them. This is a lie. Our families will finish us off!

- How will my brother Youssef react! I thought.

When I fell asleep, I dreamt he was strangling me.

More women arrived all day the next day.

Some of them had been assaulted as they got off the bus on their way home from work. The lynching continued in certain parts of the city.

Madjid, Fatiha's fiancé, also came. He cried out for vengeance:

- Fatiha, I've brought a jerry can of petrol. I'm going to blow it up, Fatiha. Do you hear me? I'm going to avenge you.

And then he sobbed:

---

14. Long tunic.

- Forgive me Fatiha, I can't marry you. Forgive me, my family will never accept. I love you Fatiha. But I can't.

Fatiha didn't answer.

More women arrived on the third day.

Some had only later been found in the dunes. Beaten and raped by several men at once, they lay unconscious on the sand, or had managed to escape.

The doctors handed out prescriptions. They put them next to our heads. We didn't understand this gesture: the women's houses had been ransacked, their clothes and papers burnt. We could no longer prove our identity. We had no money. Nothing left! To go to the bathroom, we had to cover ourselves with our blood-stained sheets. So what was the point of this charade of prescriptions? And the medical certificates that followed? Neither Fatiha nor I thought to look at them. Some of the women exclaimed in shock:

- What are these certificates?! I'm bleeding like an animal. I smell rotten from the inside. And they give me two days?

- I have zero days and can barely stand up. We haven't even seen a doctor!

No gynecologist had examined us. The worst affected, those who were still in intensive care, only received seven days' incapacity. The luckiest of the others were entitled to three days; some of us, nothing at all.

And it was already our third day in hospital.

It was too much. I put on the *gandoura* Fatema had brought me. Fatiha wanted to come with me, but as soon as she stood up, her whole body started shaking and she lost consciousness.

Accompanied by two other victims from Frenda, I entered the office of the doctor, an obstetrician from Oran, like the hospital director. She was wearing a *hijab*.

- Who made these certificates?" I asked.

- I drew them up with the hospital director.

- Do you think it's fair to give us disabilities of just seven, three or two days?

- You want to get them convicted? she retorted.

This answer left us speechless for a few moments.

- You think you're their lawyer?! Let justice do its job and do yours a little better, if possible! The women who got seven days are still in intensive care and we don't even know if they're going to survive! I finally reacted.

- You haven't even examined us, how can you make certificates? I've lost my virginity! And we can barely stand upright," added one of the women accompanying us, while I added:

- My girlfriend, who's in the same bed as me, pisses blood all over the place and she's only had three days of incapacity, just like me! Like all the others in the big room that stinks of piss, vomit and blood.

I spoke with difficulty. But I spoke.

- That's the way it's done," replied the doctor carelessly. There's nothing we can do. We didn't put you in this state.

- And it's not you who's taking care of us! You're covering up for our murderers. Just like the newspapers that say we're prostitutes! And the 65-year-old woman who suffered the same fate as us, is she a whore too?!

- Oh, but you're asking for trouble! If you're not happy, go and see the manager," she yelled.

But the man would have none of it. He wouldn't change the number of days on the certificates. As for the prescriptions and our inability to afford medication, he couldn't care less:

- That's not my problem. I'm not your father.

A journalist from *El Watan*, Salima Tlemçani, was there with some of her colleagues. She questioned us. We informed her of the way we were treated.

That night, a few beds away from me, a woman gave birth prematurely. I heard nothing. The next morning, all I could see was a tiny baby asleep in her arms.

My cousin Amar was stuck in Haoud El Hamra for two days before he managed to reach me. As were many other people trying to reach Hassi Messaoud.

The town was off-limits to civilians until calm had returned.

He explained that he was very upset: I had received him at home the day before I was attacked, asking me to lend him some money before going to Oran. We'd spent part of the afternoon together talking about the whole family. He had wanted to tell me something, but couldn't remember what it was. He remembered only after hearing about the lynching. One of his friends had warned him that there had been a preaching at the El Haïcha mosque, in which there was talk of cleansing the town of impure women. There was even a small poster on the mosque wall. He'd probably forgotten because he hadn't taken the threats seriously. He'd never imagined that the madness of men could destroy so much.

- In any case, I wouldn't have moved, since I didn't feel concerned.

I wasn't saying that to comfort him. I meant it.

I didn't feel impure.

Since we weren't being treated, we decided to leave the hospital. Management tried to stop us. But the protests became more and more violent, and the press supported us with stories of the abject way we were treated. One by one, we received our discharge orders.

We were to go to the youth hostel next to the hospital. It had been reopened especially for us on the evening of the tragedy.

22. The Inn

Under police escort, in small groups, day after day, we disembarked at this establishment. 60°C in the shade; no air-conditioning.

We were a hundred women and children. Some of the women who had managed to escape before being attacked, leaving behind their ransacked homes, had been there since the first night, it seemed. Piled on top of each other, the luckiest had beds; others, mattresses on the ground; but the majority of us slept on the ground, sometimes in the courtyard.

We were given potato sandwiches that we couldn't chew because our smashed faces were torturing us. We had no drinking water.

We were forbidden to leave the premises, except under police escort; nor could we receive visitors without authorization. The door was padlocked and guarded by a policeman.

We were under house arrest.

- Those who want to go out must have a guardian! A man, of course! we were told. Of course, we tried to protest, but we were far too weakened to fight the uniform.

On the first day, we were taken to the police station to testify, but we could hardly stand on our wobbly legs, so we were quickly escorted back to the hostel.

That night, another woman, a very young one at that, gave birth to her little one at seven months pregnant. Between the hospital and the hostel, there were three premature deliveries.

All day long, the women clung to the fences, accosting passers-by, begging them to buy them the medicines prescribed in the famous prescriptions.

After the journalists, the politicians, the heads of women's associations began to arrive.
We were introduced to Nouara Djaffar and Khalida Messaoudi, both members of parliament at the time[15]. They came to assure us of their solidarity, they told us, full of concern. They also reiterated that they would support us and not let us down.

---

15. Nouara Djaffar is currently Minister of the Family and Khalida Messaoudi has been Minister of Culture since 2002.

We were asked not to talk to journalists.

One of them leaned over Fatiha to ask how she was doing:

- Bring us back a drink first. Then you can ask me how it's going! she retorted.

- Are you that thirsty?" the politician asked.

- By now, I'd even drink your piss.

We were fed up. We explained it to anyone who would listen.

The same day, an ambulance was dispatched, with a bellyful of much-needed medicines.

But Fatiha, who was still bleeding from the chest, refused treatment:

- It took the arrival of a few officials for you to decide to treat us! We took care of ourselves the whole time. We'll keep it that way," she murmured.

Word spread through the hostel and the women supported Fatiha's position. None of the women accepted treatment, and those who could take showers disinfected each other with bleach.

A wind of revolt was rumbling.

- Why don't they let us out? We're not minors!

At night, Fatiha and I slept on a small mattress on the floor.

She shivered. In her sleep, she called me Ma, and hugged me in her emaciated arms.

Then she screamed and struggled:

- Ma, don't let me go! Ma, don't leave me!

Two or three of us would try to calm her down by hugging her tightly to our stomachs.

Sometimes it was me who woke up screaming.

We were all there; the ferocity of men haunted us all. The cries of sleeping or awake women, struggling again and again each night against the ignominy, echoed through the inn at all times.

The doctor at the base where Fatiha worked paid us a visit. Usually discreet and reserved, he fulminated against the way we were being treated. As Fatiha's wounds wouldn't close and were starting to become dangerously infected, he returned, accompanied by an Italian colleague. They treated her wounds, which now reeked of carrion. That's about all they could do for her and for us.

One day, late in the afternoon, while we were in the courtyard with some journalists, I spotted Ferièle chatting with a man. I recognized him immediately. Mohamed E'chaoui! I couldn't believe my eyes; there he was, inside the inn, chatting quietly, close to us. Even though he'd guided our attackers. My heart was racing, I tried with all my might to keep calm.

- Do you know who this man is? He's her savior," a journalist told me.

- And he's my attacker!" I replied.

Discreetly, I spoke to the policeman at the entrance, who called for back-up. I was very anxious that the man would get away. When they arrested him, Ferièle was stunned; she defended him vigorously:

- But no, I assure you that it was he who handed me a *djellaba* to cover myself up and who rescued me from the hands of my rapists to take me to hospital!

Ferièle had been assaulted late afternoon on July 14, as she was getting off her staff bus. They tore off her clothes and inserted a broomstick into her vagina. Mohamed E'chaoui rushed in and saved her. Thus, some people, realizing that the number of police had increased between the night of the 13th and the day of the 14th and that they were making arrests, went from being executioners to protectors.

After a few days, Khalida Messouadi, Nouara Djaffar and other officials called me to discuss the next steps.

They spoke in hushed tones.

A gentleman with dark brown hair, quite stout and good-looking, was asking me questions without me even knowing who he was.

That's when I received a phone call from my mother telling me that Youssef had thrown her and my daughters out after reading the newspaper. They were now staying with my sister. My sister had been forced to take a fortnight's leave when her colleagues learned that I was living in Hassi.

And all these officials were salamandizing each other around a table and didn't dare call a spade a spade.

I shouted at them with all my rage:

- Don't tell me that my ordeal is over, because it's not! My mother and daughters are out there! And no one will condemn the criminals who did this or who wrote that we were prostitutes! You want to see what they did, you want to see?!

I ripped my shirt.

My blue breasts, my blood, my scabs, I flaunted them.

I won't be fooled by modesty again.

Fatiha and Ferièle stood up behind me. They too took off their dresses. As revolted as I was.

- That's why we're all the same. It's better that you see what they've done to us. So you know what we're talking about. We came here to keep our dignity. And this is the result. And on top of that, they call us prostitutes," Fatiha told me.

- Ask women if they've been raped and they'll tell you. I don't know, I fainted. I don't know what they did to me. We came here to work. And they imprison us! We're the ones they lock up! We're going to blow the doors off!

Khalida and Nouara tried to hug us to soothe us. The man I didn't know spoke:

- We don't imprison you, we protect you. Spirits have not calmed in the city. What's more, if we open the doors, most of you will go home and the culprits will never be punished. That's not what we want. We want the culprits arrested, tried and convicted. Do the confrontations at the police station, then go home. But first, take photos of each other: the investigation is being conducted by men, we can't ask you to show us your wounds.

Khalida Messaoudi added:

- You were not treated in this hospital. And there have been no examinations. We're trying to organize the departure of all the women to Algiers so that you can be cared for by competent doctors and diagnosed in preparation for the trial. We'll be by your side and we won't let you down, I promise you. We'll fight so that you get compensation. So that no Algerian woman goes through what you have.

Under police escort, I was taken home to retrieve my camera. I also took my papers, my savings and some clothes.

Thanks to my little instamatic and a roll of film given to me by an assistant public prosecutor, we were able to take some shots and give them to him.

One morning, I took Fatiha out into the courtyard for some fresh air. We were sitting on chairs, watching the comings and goings of passers-by, when Fatiha suddenly stood still, terrified.

The man approaching also froze:

- She's not dead! The bitch has seven lives! he told his friend.

Fatiha, trembling and panicking, started screaming at the top of her lungs:

- He's the one! He's the one who killed me!

The assailant, who was trying to escape, was caught.

It was the man in the gray shirt and patched sandals.

Fatiha couldn't stop screaming, screams that pierced your soul, as if she were being slaughtered all over again.

She was taken to hospital for an injection of Valium.

Later, she returned, calm and victorious.

- They got it, they got it!

For the first time, I saw her smile again.

23. Preliminary Inquest

Confrontations at the police station have begun, in preparation for the trial.

We were brought in small groups. We waited in the corridors until we were called to record our statements.

We had to recognize our torturers. Coming face-to-face with the accused was unbearable; there was no tinted glass to separate us from their gaze, as in American films. We had to stand opposite them, in the same room. Our legs buckled, we could barely lift our eyes from our feet.

Once the ordeal was over and one of the accused had been found guilty, we returned to the offices, where we had to recount in great detail what they had done to us. They denied everything; the police beat them up as we watched. To be honest, we didn't feel sorry for them. We'd suffered too much for that. But this violent incident was impressive and shocking all the same: a policeman smashed a glass bottle over the head of a detainee he was interrogating in front of Fatiha. She left the office quite shaken.

My traumatized memory was like a jigsaw puzzle that I had to rebuild. There were a lot of missing pieces that would sometimes resurface unexpectedly. And each of them was painful. Fatiha told me she felt the same way.

One day, while I was waiting in the corridor, I saw Mohamed E'chaoui coming out of an office where he had been heard for the minutes. I jumped on him and beat him with all the force of my hatred. I would have killed him with my fists if the police hadn't separated us. And he, as if he were the most innocent man in the world:
- What's going on, Rahmouna? I've done nothing to you!
A policeman later told me that he had said about me that I was a quiet woman, respected and appreciated in the neighborhood.
My executioner!
The one who appointed me with his list and orders!

At 1pm, sandwiches and water were distributed to the victims, but not to the prisoners.
As Fatiha still couldn't eat, she headed for the inmates. As she made her way back to me, without her

sandwich or bottle of water, I saw that a policeman was gently lecturing her. She smiled as best she could with her face in lint.

- What were you thinking doing that?

- I felt sorry for him.

- You didn't show pity to any of those men when they tried to kill you," I reminded him a little curtly.

- I gave it to a guy in the next cell. I'm not stupid enough to give it to one of our murderers. Unless I put some rat poison in it, but I don't have any.

She hadn't lost her sense of humor.

Fatiha spotted her policeman neighbor as he crossed the corridor to an office, files in hand. Frozen with fear, she said nothing. She tried to understand what she was seeing; and what she was seeing made her lose confidence: this policeman, who had contemplated her torture instead of shooting in the air or calling for backup, seemed quite at home in his house. What if the whole thing was just politics?

For the time being, Fatiha preferred to be left alone with her questions rather than share them.

Madjid came to see her at the inn.

They were very emotional, but didn't speak to each other. Then, suddenly, her former fiancé exclaimed:

- Just tell me who did this to you and I'll avenge you. You certainly knew some of them. Do you remember?

I'm in pain, Fatiha. You don't know how much. I must avenge you!

- But there will be a trial, Madjid.

- I don't believe this. I want to help you.

- You can't disobey your parents and you pretend to be a savior?

After his departure, Fatiha remained prostrate on a chair for a long time.

24. A Day in Oran

I finally got my ticket; I was finally able to go to Oran. I was dying to see my daughters and mother again, but I was apprehensive about coming face to face with the rest of the family.

I arrived at my sister's house, exhausted. Ma opened the door for me. What a shock! She was skinny, but her belly was huge, as if she were nine months pregnant; she had a yellow complexion and blue bags under her eyes.

I burst into tears. She was sick and nobody had told me. She was crying too. She hugged me:

- Oh my daughter, I was so worried about you! What have we done to you, Rahmouna? And I couldn't even come to see you.

When I opened my eyes again, I saw Nacéra. She looked at me for a long time. Then she came over and kissed me. As for Hassina, she refused to approach me. She ran away as soon as I tried to join her, disappearing from one room to another.

Unable to stand, I lay down with my mother's help. She went to prepare me a small salad, which she brought to me in slow steps.

- Ma, what's wrong?

- My daughter, I don't know. I feel very tired and a fortnight ago, my belly suddenly swelled up. It hurts like hell, but I don't have time to get treatment. Your cousin is dead. We have to bury him today. I don't even have enough money to go to the funeral.

- Don't worry, Ma, you'll be fine. But you have to get treatment!

My brother Abdelhak arrived, as did my maternal uncle Ahmed. How cold their welcome was! I was devastated. That damned newspaper again! I'd borrowed money from them for the house; now I could hear them demanding it from my mother in the next room. She was outraged. I opened my shopping bag and took out the bills.

- Ma, give it to them!

My brother, seeing that this offended me, didn't want to take it, but I insisted, furious.

In the corridor, Hassina asked Nacera:

- But she wasn't dead, was she, Ma?

- They thought she was dead, but it wasn't true. You can see she's not dead.

Nacéra reassured her and brought her back to me. She snuggled into my arms and cried. I was finally able to kiss her. We stayed up until very late, my two brown angels snuggled up to me like little cats. I admired them as they talked to me. They were so pretty with their long hair and well-defined eyebrows!

My little girls who had grown up without me. What was the point of it all?

The next morning, before going to school, Hassina handed me a small empty matchbox.

- Put your perfume in it. So I can keep it with me when you're far away.

I tried not to cry to give them courage. I promised to come back very soon.

Just before leaving for Hassi, I went to a laboratory and asked to be tested for all sexually transmitted diseases, including AIDS. I was worried sick about getting it. Not knowing whether I'd been raped made me sick; everywhere I went from then on, there was this ball of anxiety that twisted my stomach and knotted my throat. I felt dirty. Only the warmth of my mother and children could comfort me. Now I'd have to go back to the inn, with its screams, tears and wounds.

I was going to have to find my attackers. I wanted them to pay. But the confrontations were very hard to bear.

25. Instruction

Fatiha's face had deepened since I'd left. And her spirits were low.

- You see, I no longer have a fiancé and no one to turn to. I called my mother and she told me not to come home. My brother has sworn to kill me if I come back. As soon as I speak to her, all she says is "your brother": "your brother won't want to; your brother will know; your brother, your brother, your brother... My daughter, I'm afraid I'll die before I see you...". That's what she told me before hanging up. If I lose my mother, all I have to do is die. I should have died rather than suffer this.

Fatiha had been very close to her brother when she was a child. As she lived alone with him and her mother, and her mother worked, it was he, Abbes, who looked after her all day. It was he who did her hair in the morning before taking her to school and her college, which was right next door. It was he who, at lunchtime, reheated the meal their mother had prepared for them the day before. She talked to him a lot. He loved to make her laugh.

At weekends, with their mother, the three of them would walk around town; and if one of them liked something, they would get it at the beginning of the month, when their mother was paid.

This period of childhood was a wonderful part of life for Fatiha, and she would take refuge in her happy memories whenever her situation became unbearable.

Everything had changed when his brother's voice had changed. He began to speak loudly. Fatiha flinched every time he called her name. From then on, he only spoke to her to give her orders and forbade her to chatter:

- A girl shouldn't talk so much with her brother," he would declare curtly. Their mother nurtured the son's authority: with the father absent, she felt it was necessary for him to play the role of dominant male and watch over the *charaf*, the family honor.

Fatiha would have liked to have had girlfriends, to play with them at home or in the street. But this was strictly forbidden. Most of her adolescence was spent in solitude.

Abbes was so overzealous that, years later, it was his mother who was startled when he shouted at her.

Powerless and tired, she would rather submit than fight him.

One day, Abbes ordered her to put the house in his name. She complied, after timidly objecting.

We heard the news that affected us all. The father of Naïma Sbâa, who had been raped by countless men, had committed suicide shortly afterwards.

The poor old man, who was an imam and could not accept what had happened to his daughter, had also had to face the gaze of the faithful who prayed in his mosque and had read the *El Khabar* newspaper. He couldn't bear it, and despite the Muslim religion's opprobrium on suicide, he had committed the irreparable act, which his daughter now had to conceal, so as not to further damage the gaze that could be cast on her name.

Nacer, Fatiha's baggage handler neighbor, came to visit her. For a long time, they stood silently next to each other, unable to look at each other, unable to utter a single word, their throats constricted. After some hesitation, he finally took Fatiha's badge out of his pocket and handed it to her:

- I found it in the sand. I glued it back together. You should have come and taken refuge with us.

- I know, but I couldn't.

- Do you need anything, Fatiha?

- No, thanks.

Nacer hesitated again. But he left without adding anything.

The Minister of Solidarity, his chief of staff and their entire staff came to our hostel. He addressed an audience of journalists and officials of all kinds:

- We are ready to help you rebuild your lives. Criminals must be punished. At the trial, you will need all your strength. So we'll support you. We will pay for your lawyers and your travel expenses. You have the right to your dignity. We'll do everything we can to help you regain it.

We warmly applauded these comforting words.

The investigation began in court at the end of July. We all went there. It was so crowded that we were all sitting on the floor, while the chairs were occupied by men we didn't know.

- Are they here on another case?" I asked a policeman.

- No. They're here on the same business as you. They're the men from the Ledjna. They've come to support the accused.

- They support the defendants, they hold the chairs and we sit on the floor. I hope the trial won't be like this...

The Ledjna was made up of presidents and representatives of neighborhood committees who were also

25. Instruction

members of our attackers' families. It was not uncommon for them to approach the victims to intimidate them into retracting their statements.

The first three or four days of the trial lasted until 3 or 4 in the morning. To my surprise, I knew the prosecutor, Mr. Nejjar.

He was the man who, at the inn, had asked me to take our picture. We went into his office, in twos and threes, one after the other. We repeated what we'd already said and rehearsed at the police station. For me, it wasn't a tiring exercise: I had the feeling that I was continuing my re-education.

We had to face our torturers again, in the office of Mr. Nejjar, the prosecutor.

When Fatiha saw her police neighbor in the courtroom, she told the prosecutor, who asked her to point him out. There was also a confrontation in his office. Fatiha blamed the policeman for not coming to her aid. Instead of watching her being torn to pieces, he could have called his colleagues for help...

- You could at least have fired a shot in the air to scare them off.

- I'm not allowed to use my weapon if I'm not on duty.

- But other police officers have done it!

- But I don't give a damn about you," retorted the policeman.

That was the end of the matter. And despite Fatiha's bitterness, the policeman was not bothered.

To the women who mentioned the imam to Mr. Nejjar, he replied evasively that his business was separate. No one understood what that meant. But in all the melee, no one thought to ask for clarification.

In all, thirty-nine of the worst-affected women agreed to lodge a complaint and attend the trial. That was so few compared with the number of women martyred and torn to shreds!

Khalida Messaoudi came to find Fatiha and me at the hostel: she wanted us to convince the women to come down to Algiers to be examined and treated. Very few women agreed, so she asked us to set an example by accompanying them.
- Are you going to cure us of the disaster the newspaper has caused our families? You must promise to bring *El Khabar* to justice.
- We'll do everything we can.

Just before we went down to Algiers, the big boss of the company where Fatiha worked asked to see her. With Ferièle's help, we washed her hair, still full of blood and dirt.

When she got out of the Toyota that had been sent to pick her up, all her colleagues were there to greet her: they all expressed their solidarity and sympathy.

The boss, along with two other managers and a translator, received her in his office. It was the first time she had met him. He asked about her health and her needs; he asked for more medicines to be ordered and sent to her; he provided her with shampoo, towels and shower gel. It wasn't much, but these little gestures touched her deeply.

When she came out, they were still waiting for her: her colleagues knew she'd lost everything; they'd taken up a collection and handed her the envelope before wishing her good luck.

When she returned, Fatiha was delighted, full of enthusiasm. She could go back to work, she told me. Maybe we'd even put her up on the base. That way, she would no longer be prey for her attackers! What else could she do, since she was forbidden to return home?

It was the first time I'd heard him talk about a possible future. It reassured me.

26. Darna and Ma's Disease

It was Fatiha's first time on a plane. She was even paler than usual, and stubbornly refused to get out of her seat even though a pressing urge was torturing her.

From Algiers airport, we were driven to Darna, the refuge center of the Rachda association[16]. It was a large center with chalets containing rooms shared by two of us, while a large kitchen enabled us all to meet up at mealtimes, which we took turns preparing for each other.

When we arrived, we were given towels, shampoo, soap and sheets. It was a big difference from the hostel. Despite these comforts, which I hadn't experienced in a long time, I was still worried. I'd had my mother on the phone earlier in the day:

- Your daughters joined Hamid in Laayoune for a short vacation. It's better this way," she told me.

---

16. The Rassemblement contre la Hogra et pour les droits des Algériennes works to defend the moral and material interests of women.

She seemed at the end of her rope. I wanted to see her.

The next morning, after a good shower, as the women were getting ready to go to hospital for tests, I announced my departure for Oran.

My sister Baya told me that our mother had returned home. This meant I had to confront my brother. It didn't matter, I had to see her.

Khadija opened the door for me; she didn't greet me. It hurt. Two of my three youngest sisters hadn't been allowed to work and hadn't married: they'd never been asked and, as they were forbidden to go out, they'd never met any men likely to marry them. They were dependent on Youssef, whom they served like a pasha, submitting to his conditions and acquiescing to everything he said and thought, I suppose.

My mother was lying on the floor of her bedroom. She was burning with fever.

She had pissed herself. I helped her into the bathroom for a shower. I thought it would help bring the fever down. As I soaped her belly, I felt a big lump, like a large stone.

I understood immediately.

The sky, with all its weight, was falling on my head. But I didn't want to cry in front of her.

- Ma, I'll take care of you and you'll come and live with me in my house.

- And which house, my daughter?" she said, smiling sadly.

- I'll go back to Hassi and finish building it with the money I've earned.

- God willing," she replied, not really believing it.

I wanted to kiss her, squeeze her, hold her.

My God, don't let her die!

I hated my sisters for not taking care of her. I hated my brother because he had thrown her out on the street.

- Tomorrow morning, I'll take you to the doctor.

- You're sick, my girl, take care of yourself.

- No, Ma. You're the one who's sick.

That night, I pressed my foam mattress against her bed. I wanted to sleep next to her and smell her, like a little girl.

I asked a neighbor to accompany us to the gastroenterologist who was treating me.

We spent two hours in consultation. He was perplexed.

- Why didn't you bring her in sooner?

- She wasn't there," justified my mother.

- She needs emergency surgery. Take her directly to the hospital.

He wrote a letter and, with it clutched between my fingers, we rushed to the emergency room. At no point had he uttered the word *tumor*. I remained hopeful.

26. Darna And Ma's Disease

She had to undergo the operation during the night, unwillingly:

- If they open the door, I die, so I might as well die at home.

While she was waiting to be taken to the operating room, she wanted to go to the bathroom. As I helped her to her feet, a foul-smelling liquid gushed from her belly, and I couldn't figure out how. I was drenched. A stench invaded my throat. Surprised, I jumped back and fled the room, completely panicked. I called for a nurse.

- That's it, you've disowned me," whispered my mother as we both entered her room.

Pus, then blood, in abundance, leaked from her torn belly. The nurses and I plugged the wound with compresses and bandages.

We took it to the OR.

That's when I heard the surgeon drop the fateful word *tumor*. The earth crumbled beneath my feet.

Ma was dying.

Why was God so against me? I was alone, so alone. I phoned my sisters; they weren't going to come in the middle of the night, they said. I was stunned. I left the cabin, distraught. I vomited and vomited and vomited until I bled.

When he woke up in the morning, Ma made me promise to take care of my brother Abdelhak and, above all, never to sue my brother Youssef.

- Swear on the Koran that you won't sue him, whatever happens.

The surgeon told me he was going to try another operation.

I gave my mother a big kiss before leaving her, promising to return very soon.

I thought of all that pus dripping from her belly like so much accumulated sadness and bitterness she could no longer contain.

I returned to Darna.

On August 7, 2001, Pr Janine Benkhodja, gynecologist and obstetrician, carried out a complete check-up of each of us at the Bab El Oued University Hospital in preparation for the trial. When she heard about us, she offered her services. She was a petite woman in her fifties, whose gentleness and delicate gestures reconciled us with all humanity, despite the difficulty of confronting such a clinical examination.

From the cabinet, two of the women we examined let out yelps of relief; we understood that they were still virgins. They had a few local lesions, but the rape attempts had been unsuccessful.

However, not all were so lucky: three of us had been deflowered during the rape. The young women were inconsolable, despite all our words of appeasement. How would their families receive this news? How would they prove to them that the loss of their virginity was not their fault?

It's been that way for us women for generations: our honor and that of our entire lineage lies right between our thighs.

None of the thirteen women taking refuge in Darna had sexually transmitted diseases.

Twenty-one days after our assaults, we all had obvious lesions. And all of us still had traces of the knife wounds and scratches that marred our breasts.

Sodomy for one of them, who had suffered a severe haemorrhage, requiring stitches which Pr Benkhodja removed.

I hadn't been raped. The news left me speechless. In the depths of my being, the savagery of the acts had been such that it was as good as done.

I took advantage of my stay in Darna to try and gather my strength to return to work in Hassi.

During a lunch with Khalida Messaoudi, we received a surprise visit from the Minister of Maghreb and African Affairs, Mr Abdelkader Messahel, who told us:

- I'm not here in my capacity as Minister, but on behalf of the President of the Republic, Abdelaziz Bouteflica. He has asked me to give you this envelope of 260,000 dinars, to be divided between the thirteen of you. I should point out that he hasn't touched any taxpayers' money, but that this sum is part of his personal fund. I'll need to return with your files, as the Chairman has requested them in order to intervene personally in this matter.

We were all moved: this sum was important for all of us. On the one hand, the women could hope to find other gurbis to rent than their devastated homes; on the other hand, the president had heard of us and was not insensitive to our case. If he intervened, we'd be saved!

I immediately thought that, with this money, I could help my mother get better. I'd be able to leave my children with my sister for a few more months, just long enough to see them through; and above all, just long enough for my mother to recover, *insha'Allah*!

Darna was always full: all kinds of officials visited us to express their solidarity and promise to help us. This cheered us up, in addition to the antidepressants and tranquilizers we were given in high doses every day.

Between the image of my mother, her face ravaged by illness, and the nightmarish vision of my aggressors, it was the only thing that could relieve me of my deep distress. A psychologist also came every day; and every day, Fatiha had a session with her. I categorically refused; I preferred, as the saying goes, to leave the well with its lid on. If I started talking, I felt like I was going to implode.

26. Darna and Ma's Disease

We were told that we were to have a collective of nine lawyers and that we had to start preparing for the trial with them: four or five of them came to question us every day and listen to us tell each of our stories in great detail. They took photos and medical certificates. They seemed highly motivated and pumped us up: as far as they were concerned, we could not fail to be heard in our demand for reparation.

After each interview with the lawyers, we spoke with the heads of the associations. We wanted this trial to set an example so that never again, in any region of Algeria, would a woman be attacked.

We were beginning to believe it.

Before going back to my mother, I went to Hassi to make sure my job was still vacant. As I only had a fixed-term contract, I wanted to show my presence so that the bosses wouldn't forget me. A woman replaced me for a month, so I was reassured.

As the antidepressants began to take their toll on the women, Fatiha and the others soon decided to return to Hassi Messaoud.

27. Fatiha Returns to Hassi

At the end of August 2001, the mayor and the commissioner welcomed the women returning from Darna at the airport.

They had lunch with them in a popular snack bar emptied for the occasion. The tension was palpable. Everyone feared a possible attack. Police officers stood at the entrance. They hurriedly dispatched the meal and went to the town hall for the passes.

But how were they going to get back to work in this atmosphere? Fatiha, more than ever, wanted to get busy: change the sheets, dust, put everything back in its place. Quickly. Quickly to finish the twenty-two rooms in her care on time. Empty the garbage cans, scrub the shower and the WC in the bathroom. Mopping the floor. These tasks, which once wearied her, she now wanted to repeat over and over again. To be nothing more than an automaton and, above all, to let no image cross her mind. Those dozens of voracious hands, those bloodshot eyes fixed on her, those dirty biting teeth, those bellowing mouths. No more! Never again!

When she arrived at Eurest, the subcontracting company that employed her for Schlumberger, an Italian oil base, she took out her badge and handed it to the security guard, announcing herself and asking to see Brahim, the personnel manager.

It was he who had hired her and allowed her to sign a permanent contract, seeing her so zealous at work. But his assailants, along with all her papers, had also burned her contract. She'd ask him for a new copy, she thought, while the security guard called Brahim. But he announced:

- Monsieur Brahim cannot see you now.
- When can he?" she asked naively.
- He didn't tell me.
- Well, you'll have to ask him," she replied without flinching.

The security guard looked weary and called again. This didn't bode well: security guards often mime their bosses' moods, and his wasn't very encouraging.

Brahim categorically refused to receive her, to come down to talk to her or to take her on the phone. He advised her to find a job elsewhere.

Fatiha's head began to swirl. It was all well and good: the welcoming committee, the passes issued by the mayor himself, the warm handshakes; but then what? Good luck and get on with it! That's how it always ended.

What was she going to do now? She didn't know where to go. She wandered around Hassi Messaoud for hours in the middle of August, head down to avoid the stares of the men who now terrorized her.

The fear of losing her footing nagged at her.

She wanted to see her mother.

And then, sudden anguish: she'd been walking down the street for too long; what if someone recognized her?

Now she was almost running. Like a hunted beast. She made her way to the bus station. Too bad, might as well go for it.

She took a bus to Tiaret. One thousand one hundred kilometers later, she called her mother:

- Ma, it's me, I'm in Tiaret. Let me come and see you, please!

- My daughter, why did you do that?! Don't come all the way here!" cried her distraught mother.

- Ma, I miss you. I need you... Come on, you. I'll wait for you at the bus station. He won't know.

- I can't help you. I'd so much like to help you, my daughter. But if he found out, he'd never forgive me.

- Ma, ya Ma, I beg you," Fatiha sobbed.

His mother was upset, but didn't want to know.

So, with the president's money, Fatiha bought a ticket to return to Hassi.

27. Fatiha Returns to Hassi

She searched desperately for her former fiancé. But he was nowhere to be found. By dint of getting lost in the streets, she came across a friend of his, Ayachi. She hardly knew him, but recognizing a familiar face in the city did her good. He too was from the West.

Madjid said of Ayachi that he was a son of a good family and not one to make trouble or meddle in other people's affairs.

- Fatiha, I know what happened to you. I'm really sorry. If there's anything I can do to help, please let me know.

- Marry me," she said, staring him straight in the eyes.

She herself was stunned by these words, which echoed in her head as if they had come from another mouth. This was the first time she had ever asked a man to marry her. Her audacity was the audacity of desperation. If he said no, she'd dig a hole right here and disappear forever, she decided.

He, too, was receiving this type of request for the first time. He blushed.

- Why do you want me to marry you? Weren't you engaged to Madjid?" he asked sincerely.

She hadn't expected this question as an answer.

So she explained everything. The diary, the break-up with Madjid, her brother's death threats, her vanished job. And the vital need to find her mother, the only person in the world who understood her.

- I can't find any work and I'm too hot. I think I'll go home. Would you like to come with me to my family?" he finally asks her.

It wasn't done at all, but she accepted.

28. Fatiha's Wedding

Ayachi's parents were very conservative former farmers, like the rest of the inhabitants of the village of Rjem Demmouch, located one hundred and twenty kilometers from Sidi Bel Abbès, on the Moroccan border, and close to a huge colonial-era barracks. During the day, most of the population was made up of military personnel; the dwellings were former settlers' cottages, extended with odds and ends, or unfinished new constructions, sometimes for lack of money, often out of superstition: it's best not to finish building your house, so as not to attract the evil eye of the envious.

In this remote corner of the world, where the grocery store is also the bakery and butcher's shop, all the neighbors are uncles, aunts or cousins. Most are unemployed and are taken in by those who have jobs. Women rarely go out without a *hijab*, and it's frowned upon for them to work.

Fatiha's arrival in this small world of traditions was not well received. Ayachi introduced her as a colleague he didn't want to leave on the road alone.

- Doesn't this colleague have a family? And if she does, why is she so far from home?

After three or four days of cohabitation, Ayachi announced to Fatiha that he was now ready to hit the road again to propose to her older brother. He hadn't hesitated for long: he'd had a crush on her since the first day he met her, but hadn't dared declare his love for her, out of respect for his friend Madjid.

- In a way, it hurts me that we're getting married in this context. But I tell myself that if God made us meet in Hassi when we were both very unhappy, it's perhaps because he wanted to give us a fresh start, here on earth.

He told his family that he would accompany Fatiha home so she wouldn't get lost or meet the wrong people.

Fatiha's mother wouldn't open the door; she spoke through the door, her voice broken by tears.

- Your brother's here, girl, what are you doing? Have you come to die?

Fatiha was sobbing too:

- Open the door, open the door, Ma! He won't kill me. I've come to tell him I'm getting married. The man who is to marry me is here. He wants to talk to him.

28. Fatiha's Wedding

- Oh my God, my daughter, he's going to kill people's children too!

There was silence, then the door hinges groaned.

The brother appeared.

He was crushing her with his gaze.

Fatiha wished she'd been braver. But she couldn't do it. He had never frightened her so much, this brother who had so amused her when they were little.

Now she was trembling, her face flooded with tears.

- I've come with a son of the family who wants to marry me according to the rules of religion," she said hastily.

- Follow me," he ordered Ayachi, after staring at him for a moment.

They locked themselves in a room for a long time; mother and daughter, on the other side of the wall, watched for the slightest suspicious noise.

When they reappeared, his brother decreed:

- The wedding is tomorrow. In the morning, you'll convince your father about the guardianship.

- Yes, brother," she nodded, not daring to look at him.

It's all right, these humiliations, she thought. I'll be able to see Ma again. That's all I need.

No white dress, no show, just a little couscous eaten in the deathly silence imposed by her brother: that's how Fatiha got married.

But she didn't care.

She belonged to this family again, and found in her mother's eyes the tenderness and comfort she had sorely missed.

29. Ma Must Die

After several operations, the doctors could no longer hide the seriousness of Ma's condition. They now relied on Allah.

I was beginning to painfully accept the fatal outcome. But Ma, even though she was in pain all over her body, didn't feel ready:

- I've spawned a tribe of tramps and I'm going to die without being able to help them.

The tramps were us, her children. She was very worried. How were we going to manage without her, when none of us really had a stable situation?

- Don't let them put me in their fridge. It freezes the soul and makes you cold. After I die, I want to be warm, just a little warmer," she told me one night.

The rest of the time, she kept repeating,

- I'm going to die, without being able to leave you anything, except this cursed house that hasn't brought us luck. You need me more than ever. I can't leave you.

One morning, she asked me:

- What are you going to do with your kids?

- You're not dead yet, Ma, don't worry.

She stared sadly into my eyes:

- I'm going to die.

Suddenly, she grabbed my index finger and squeezed it hard:

- Will you die with me?

- I can't, Ma!

I tore my finger from his tight embrace and rushed out of the room, frozen. I don't know why his request upset me so much. Maybe because I realized how terrifying it is to be alone when you're dying. Maybe because part of me wanted to go with him. Maybe, quite simply, I didn't want her to go.

When I returned ten minutes later, Ma was dead. I didn't think it would be so sudden. I could still feel her hand around my finger. I thought I'd have time to say things to her. I cried my eyes out.

I stopped them from taking her into the cold room. I took her back to her house.

On the day of her *djanaza, there were* lots of people: neighbors, family and friends had come to share her couscous. My father was also present. Accompanied by

29. Ma Must Die

his last wife; even Ma had passed away, he continued to disrespect her.

This house had become unbearable for me. After the ceremony, which we paid for with the president's money, I took my three children and told my paternal uncle I was going back to Hassi.
- Don't take your children with you. Leave them with me. We'll take care of them until you find a better solution.
He lent me 800 dinars for the trip.

I arrived late in Tiaret, as there was no bus to Hassi Messaoud before dawn. So I spent the night in the bus station, populated by soldiers, homeless people and other *zawalias* like me, their faces burnt by the sun and misery.
My solitude weighed on me and frightened me.
Since July 13, I'd stopped praying and didn't even think about turning to God for help.
There was silence between us.

30. Going back to Work

In October 2001, I returned to work with relief. My colleagues were very supportive. I returned to live with Fatema. She gave me news of the other women. Some stopped coming back. Others went back to work. But what shook me the most was that my friend Zaza had completely lost her footing. She wandered around the city in rags. She talked to herself, her mind visibly tormented. Sometimes we'd find her chained to the bumper of a car. Kids' jokes that made people laugh, they said.

I didn't have the courage to go looking for him. My burden was heavy enough...

Shortly after my arrival, my children called me. They felt uncomfortable at their old uncle's house; they didn't know him very well.

So, without asking anyone's advice, they returned to my sister Baya's house, where they had always lived. So much so, in fact, that Hamid no longer obeyed her. Baya kept phoning me to complain about my son, but also to tell me about Hassina's level of schooling, which had suddenly plummeted, even though she had been a very good pupil up until then. Their behavior worried me: their grandmother, to whom they devoted unbounded affection, had died so recently! And I, their mother, wasn't there to help them through it. I resisted the guilt by convincing myself that it was this sacrifice that would finally give us our home. If I left Hassi without it being finished, all those years of effort would have been wasted.

But if I could, while waiting for our house, gather my children around me!

Fatiha had only recently arrived in Hassi. She had very few friends and hadn't put on much weight since last time. She told me about her new life with her in-laws and her psychotherapy, which was giving her some relief from her nightmares. We were happy to meet up again.

She rented a small room in an inn until she could find work. The problem was, she was so terrified of running into her attackers that her search was minimal and fruitless.

To improve our living conditions, we decided to ask for an audience with the head of the *daïra, a* native of southern Algeria.

Cold and distant, she shook our hands with her fingertips and asked us to sit down, saying she didn't have much time for us.

While the lady with the painted nails and over-loaded diary scribbled little geometric shapes on her white sheet, I did my utmost to explain my situation.

She's a woman like us," I said to myself to give myself courage, "she'll understand us.

And without restraint, I told him about my dead mother, my children on the other side of the country, whom I didn't bring back for fear of reprisals against them, my friend with whom I was staying and whom I was afraid of endangering because I had filed a complaint. The same goes for Fatiha, who was holed up in her hostel.

We'd like to have social housing away from the neighborhoods where we were attacked," I finally said.

There were plenty of them in the city, very secure; they were sprouting up like mushrooms.

It was only then that she came to life, but her answer was definitive: housing wasn't just handed out to the first people who came along. There were lists, and local residents had priority. She invited us to apply in the North.

- Algiers, for example. Severe flooding has just occurred in Bab El Oued. Prefabricated apartments have been provided for families in distress. We read

30. Going back to Work

about it in the papers this morning. Put yourself on the list. Maybe one will be allocated to you.

Was she fucking with us?

- But we were attacked in Hassi Messaoud and we don't work in Algiers!" exclaimed Fatiha.

- All I can do is give you these food vouchers for semolina and oil, which you can collect from the town hall warehouse. A small gift from the *daïra* for the month of Ramadan El Moubarik.

She accompanied this last sentence with a sympathetic chuckle.

Fatiha kindly refused:

- I'm sorry, but I'd rather not. I wouldn't know where to put them. As you know, I don't have a house.

She was disgusted and informed me of her decision to return to her in-laws the very next day.

During the night, my sister Baya called in a panic: Nacéra had come down with a terrible sore throat, accompanied by a very high fever.

The next morning, I decided to give up this life in Hassi Messaoud. I handed in my resignation, collected my children and took them to our house.

Our future haven of peace, which was so many oaths of a better tomorrow for me and my little ones, was just an interrupted building site open to the four winds.

Without doors or windows.

There was no water either. As for electricity, we got it from one of the few poles in the area. In this place, which cruelly reminded me of my broken promises, I fasted for two weeks.

31. The First Trial

On June 16, 2002, I arrived in Ouargla, *wilaya* of Hassi Messaoud, at 2pm. The closer I got to the courthouse, the more nervous I became. From a distance, I recognized the correspondent from the daily *Le Soir d'Algérie*. This familiar, friendly face reassured me, as did the presence of the press: journalists had helped us a great deal by denouncing the abject. They had also tried to rehabilitate us by explaining that we were not prostitutes, but workers. Unfortunately, it wasn't our families, of modest origins, who read the French-language newspapers.

- The journalists are here," I told Saïda from *Soir d'Algérie*.

- No, Rahmouna, the journalists aren't here. I'm the only one who made the trip.

I tried to hide my disappointment in the form of a joke:

- I hope at least the lawyers are there?

- Rahmouna, you don't have lawyers.

- Yes, we have nine.

- Rahmouna, I'm sorry, they didn't come.

- I don't know anything about it! Tell me what you know," I said, frozen by the news.

- You were supposed to have a local lawyer who was contacted three days ago, but she backed out. A lawyer was dispatched at the last minute last night, but the girls refused to let him plead because he knows nothing about the case.

Under Algerian law, it doesn't matter if victims don't have lawyers to defend them, the trial can still go ahead.

I began to panic.

- And the culprits?

- If you only knew... She sighed. They have fifteen lawyers and all their families with them who fill the room alone. They feel strong. They laugh and communicate with their loved ones without a problem. The families approach the women, harass them and threaten them with another July 13 if they don't withdraw their complaints or forgive them.

This news came as one shock after another, shattering my hopes. I no longer had the courage to enter the courthouse. I wandered around the city, distraught. What had happened to the highly motivated lawyers we had met in Darna? And all the promises made by the Minister of Solidarity, politicians and associations?

31. The First Trial

Everyone had abandoned us. They were handing us over to our attackers a second time.

Later, at the hotel, I found Nadia and Djamila, completely shaken. The three of us took a room together and they told me all about it.

Out of the crowd of five hundred men who had attacked us, there were only twenty-nine defendants; ironically, this was already too many for them: the arrogance of the defendants and their families was unrestrained; nobody called them to order. The trial seemed to be a foregone conclusion, and they sniggered as if it were all a charade.

Nadia and Djamila were among the first to take the stand. In the courtroom, those close to our murderers hurled insults and threats; intimidating little phrases flew here and there:

- If you talk, you die! Bitch, what you went through was just the beginning, next time we'll finish you off!

A defendant put his thumb to his throat and stared them straight in the eye.

Overcome by terror, the women, almost all of whom were present that day, didn't respond when the judge called their names. They slipped away as unobtrusively as possible, hoping not to be rushed outside and, above all, imploring to be forgotten forever.

Nadia and Djamila, for their part, bitterly regretted having answered the judge's call.

- I was defiled by sixty men and the judge didn't even charge me with rape. You'd have thought it was just a small demonstration with a few minor outbursts," Nadia told me.

Djamila added:

- That's our country, they hate women too much. Wherever we go, from top to bottom, it's the same, they hate us. Why should the judge be any different?

The next morning, on my way to the bus station, I met Fatiha and her mother who had just arrived.

She had received her summons the day before the trial. Ayachi, her husband, didn't want her to go; he was too afraid for her. He refused to go with her to be lynched a second time, he told her.

She had been waiting for this trial for almost a year! She was going to miss it! She called her mother to ask her to come with her. The same day, she went to her mother's house. She had to pass through Sidi Bel Abbès, then change buses for Saïda. As it was already late, she slept in the family home. At 6 a.m., the two women boarded a bus for Tiaret, where they had to take another bus to Ouargla. Hours of waiting! Hours during which Fatiha was consumed from the inside: missing her trial because the summons arrived too late, she couldn't accept.

Now she stood before me, full of anger and frustration. But when I told her about our legal woes, she no longer regretted her absence from the trial. And when

I told her that there were only twenty-nine defendants, she replied, with a bitter smile:

- Between all of us, we could have gutted them, don't you think?

When, a week later, we read the verdict, we were appalled. Of the twenty-nine defendants, three were sentenced to three years' imprisonment, sixteen to one year's imprisonment for assembling a crowd, and ten were acquitted. Among the latter was one of Fatiha's torturers, the man in the grey shirt and patched sandals. With the paper crumpled between her trembling, convulsing hands, she kept repeating, bewildered:

- Innocent! Innocent!

Mad with rage, we sought out the public prosecutor's office. We were met by his assistant, who told us that the public prosecutor had been so incensed by the ruling that he had filed an appeal and ordered a change of venue.

This news calmed us down a little. But only for a short time! I was now dreading justice and the courts.

In two round trips between Aïn Beïda and Ouargla, I'd already spent a lot of money on transport, which I'd borrowed from my sister in order to finish the month with my children. Now I'd be short, and we weren't eating at every meal.

I was hoping, and had my whole family hoping, for a letter from the Arzew oil base. Indeed, the Minister of Energy, Chakib Khalil, through his chief of staff, Mrs. Benaziza, had promised to ensure that each of the assaulted women would find a job in her home town or town of her choice: it was just a question of organization, we were told. While we waited for them to get organized, I submitted job applications to various companies throughout the region.

Despite my great anxiety, I reassured my children as best I could about our near future, and kept telling my daughters that their only salvation was school, and that nothing, nothing, must ever distract them from their studies and the opportunities they would open up for them.

The Minister had also promised to house women wishing to return to Hassi Messaoud at the bases where they would be employed, so that they would no longer have to worry about them.

It was around this time that Opgi allocated me an apartment. I'd had a contact at the allocation office for some time, the cousin of a friend's neighbor whom I'd been pestering regularly. It paid off, and I got a two-bedroom apartment, which I occupied very quickly.

Nevertheless, the situation remained difficult. I sold my house at a loss. The debts I'd incurred in building it were being claimed from me. I also had to pay a deposit and months of rent.

32. Fatiha's Battle to Get Back to Work

Ayachi's mother did not accept his marriage to Fatiha, which had taken place without her consent, which she would never have given: she blamed her son for marrying a woman who had already been married and was therefore not a virgin. What's more, as neither Fatiha nor her husband worked, they were dependent on her in-laws.

Fatiha's mother tried to help as much as she could, but it wasn't enough. So, for some time, the young woman had been trying to convince Ayachi to look for work elsewhere.

- Since you can't find a job in your hometown, and a working woman is frowned upon, why don't we get out of here? I can't stand it anymore when your mother watches what I eat at mealtimes and gives me stale bread to finish while you eat fresh bread. She spends her time rationing my water, soap and electricity. It's like wartime.

- Don't hold it against her," Ayachi excused her. My mother is a bit petty, but she's not mean. Besides, my parents are poor.

- So let's help them," she said indignantly. Let's get a job. At my mother's or in Hassi. If we both leave, it'll be easier!

But Ayachi found it dishonorable to leave his old parents to live with his mother-in-law. As for Hassi, he nicknamed it "Hell's Gate", reflecting the terror it inspired in him: the climate was too harsh and a second punitive expedition was not impossible.

On her return from the trial, Fatiha, more motivated than ever, tried to communicate her determination: they could have two good salaries thanks to which they could live better and maybe even buy a house! To be self-sufficient! She told him, despite the failure of her first attempt, that she would be scouting again the next day, and that he would just have to join her later.

- Anyway, I'm going, whether you like it or not!

This sentence sent Ayachi into a rage. But it took more than that to impress Fatiha, who had packed her shopping bag and was determined to leave.

Except her papers were gone. All her papers. Including the pass without which she couldn't return to Hassi. Furious, she threatened to divorce him if he didn't return them. But he would have none of it. Fatiha phoned her brother; four hours later, he arrived, accompanied by his mother.

32. Fatiha's Battle to Get Back to Work

The marital dispute turned into an extraordinary family reunion: it was the first time the two families had met.

Abbes tried to act as a civilized mediator and re-establish communication between the couple by addressing Ayachi:

- Fatiha is a little impulsive, but it upsets her that you have to support your family like this. She's ready to look for work herself and return to Hassi Messaoud if necessary. If you don't agree, find a solution quickly. After all, you're the man.

- Repudiate her, she loves the street too much," Fatiha's mother-in-law told her son.

- No way," retorted Ayachi. Mind your own business.

Abbes then turned to his sister:

- Can I talk to you alone?

She headed for her room, he followed, shut the door and punched her in the face. She wobbled and fell to her knees.

- If you're called a street girl, the dishonor falls on us. Don't be stronger than your husband, you're embarrassing us all, stupid! he shouted before slamming the door.

She lay prostrate on the floor of her room for hours, crying her eyes out. Much later, when there were no more tears, dying became the only thing that mattered to her. That's when Ayachi gently entered.

He sat down beside her. He placed his papers close to her hand.

- I'm so sorry. I never thought... Forgive me. Go now. Do what you have to do. But don't leave me.

Fatiha used to hate Hassi Messaoud, but this time she quickly found a job there, in a *catering* company.

It was the middle of summer 2002. The heat was at its hottest.

She rented a small studio in 136, one of the three neighborhoods hit on July 13, doubled her dose of tranquilizers and began again that old life of toil, dust and sweat.

She put the word out in her company and all over town to let her know if any positions became available for Ayachi. She missed him and was saddened by his inability to live his story: she could hardly bear his touch. And despite assiduous psychotherapy sessions a hundred and twenty kilometers from home, despite anxiolytics, she couldn't cope; as soon as he approached her, it was the eyes of his aggressors that haunted her and abruptly pulled her away from him. Most of the time, she slept only with the light on, and only if she had swallowed her sleeping pills. She would then fall into a comatose sleep, without dreams or nightmares. The next morning, she would wake up in an opaque fog.

That's how she managed to work. That's how she managed to survive.

32. Fatiha's Battle to Get Back to Work

From then on, Fatiha wore the *hijab* and even a veil to conceal her face. In Hassi, but also in all the towns she visited.

After three months, she finally landed a job for Ayachi at another base, Hassi Berkine, three hundred kilometers from Hassi Messaoud. It was terribly far away, their vacations never fell at the same time, but it would allow them to earn two salaries. After forty-two days' work, Ayachi would join his wife in Hassi Messaoud for her twenty-one days' rest; as for Fatiha, she couldn't meet Ayachi at the base when she was on leave: only men were allowed.

So, to keep her in-laws from gossiping, she would go to their house with her arms full of gifts, like a *hadja* returning from Mecca. She would then make a substantial contribution to the household chores and expenses, in order to soften her mother-in-law's resentment. Relations calmed down and Fatiha even began to enjoy family life. She regained some semblance of balance and self-confidence.

Six months later, while Fatiha was at home and Ayachi, on leave, was out with a friend, she heard loud banging on the door and window. Terrified, she screamed. Someone was trying to break down her door! The neighbor alerted Ayachi on his cell phone, who, in a Toyota, sped off in pursuit of the assailants, who fled; this time, with the help of the friend, they caught one of them and dragged him off to the police station. Fatiha followed, still trembling.

On the spot, against all odds, the police told them they weren't going to monopolize an entire police station to deal with her and her assaults. They had other things to worry about!

This was too much for Ayachi; when they were finally able to enjoy a joint vacation, when their stay with their family came to an end, he told her they would not be returning to Hassi. He was afraid for her, but also for himself: it was all right to miss his family, and the climate was unbearable; but to risk their lives, no!

Fatiha, devastated by the news, put all her energy into convincing him that this was a serious mistake. The idea of going back to square one, living off his in-laws and his mother like a parasite, horrified him even more than the possibility of another attack. She cried, she screamed, but for him it was out of the question to return to the furnace and the threats.

However, Ayachi's decision was soon shaken by a piece of news: Fatiha discovered she was pregnant. The mother-in-law, on this day, became annoyed with her son:

- How long do you think we're going to keep you all going, with a third mouth to feed? Maybe it's time you went to work!

32. Fatiha's Battle to Get Back to Work

For once, they agreed. Ayachi reluctantly returned to Hassi, accompanied by Fatiha, who was worried that they wouldn't get their jobs back.

Her fears were well founded. The recruiter wouldn't even see them. They looked for work elsewhere for almost a month, before deciding to return to square one.

It was then that the second trial took place.

33. The Second Trial

It was a long way to get to the court in Biskra. Fatiha, myself and Nadia, the third victim who had agreed to testify at the new trial in 2003, first passed through Algiers, to Darna, where the head of the Rachda association welcomed us and reassured us that we really would have lawyers this time, at least two. She had contacted them herself. We arrived in the evening in south-east Algeria, on the eve of the trial.

But the next morning in court, our lawyers weren't there. We felt terribly alone. Alone and helpless: how could we win, if this time again, no one was defending us? And why did so many people, officials, women's associations, the prosecutor himself, claim to support us if they were going to let us down at a crucial moment, crucial for us, for our honor, for that of all the women of Algeria, as they so eloquently put it, from the depths of their gilded offices? Only Halim Sahraoui, a filmmaker who was making a documentary about us at the time, was there to film our immense solitude.

There were only three defendants in the courtroom. Probably certain of their fate since the judgment in the first trial, the other defendants had not seen fit to come forward. Likewise, those who were present had not seen fit to hire a lawyer, especially as they were accompanied by their families and a dozen or so Lejna men, as impressive and intimidating as ever.

The judges called us in and asked us to sit down. We complied, humble before the justice of our country. One of the judges leaned towards his colleagues, speaking in a low voice, and even with our ears open we couldn't make out a single word. Soon, all the judges and the prosecutor himself were whispering amongst themselves. The senior judge finally exclaimed, in the direction of the defendants:

- How come you don't have any lawyers? You know very well that without lawyers, we can't go to court. I'm adjourning the case and, next time, make sure you have lawyers! The meeting is adjourned.

Fatiha and I tried to speak up, to defend our case, to explain that, after all, we didn't have lawyers either; but the judge interrupted us:

- Be quiet! I didn't ask you to speak! Meeting adjourned!

A leaden blanket fell over my shoulders. I was exhausted. My heart was pounding. I couldn't stand up. We were waiting so long to be heard! We were waiting so long to speak out against the infamy! Justice at last!

Behind me, there was a loud noise. Fatiha had collapsed. When she didn't regain consciousness, we called for an ambulance. Nadia couldn't stop crying.

Rachda's president was dismayed. She couldn't understand why the lawyers weren't there: had they been pressured? Did they consider themselves under-paid? We didn't know.

Nadia, who couldn't find a job and no longer had a permanent address, came to stay with me to rest for a while.

Fatiha, more despondent than ever, returned to her in-laws. And me, back to my job as a cook, earning a miserable 6,000 dinars. To think that I used to earn 20,000! But I had to keep going: for my children, my only reason for living.

34. Government Bureaucracy Merry-Go-Round

Shortly afterwards, I lost the job. I couldn't stand asking for money left and right. I was ashamed.

For her part, Fatiha's mother-in-law wanted to throw her and her husband out of the house. All in all, the three of us were at our wits' end.

So we decided to pay a little visit to some of the politicians who had showered us with promises. Fatiha borrowed money to get to my place, and then we took the train to Algiers.

We hadn't been able to buy tickets. We were checked en route. The carriage was packed. All eyes were on us. We handed over our identity cards. Fatiha was red-faced with shame. Anger rose from the depths of my guts:

- It's not our place to be ashamed! We'd like to pay for our tickets!" I shouted.

The Minister of Solidarity was kind enough to receive us.

The meeting lasted ten minutes. Warm, smiling and prompt, he promised to unblock the situation that had gone on for far too long.

- My chief of staff will follow up the matter. Let him know what you need. We'll come up with a solution. And don't worry, we'll give instructions to the *walis* of your respective cities.

- You promised us lawyers. We don't have any. Rachda does what she can but, at the last minute, they don't come. And each trip costs us a fortune," Fatiha revolted.

- Report the problem to my chief of staff. He'll sort it out. Don't worry," replied the Minister.

His chief of staff handed us fifty kilos of lentils and asked us to return home to await the summons from our *wilayas*.

Of course, we needed these supplies, but how could we transport these big bags? We were only able to take a few kilos, and left the rest to Darna.

A month later, we still hadn't received any invitations, and no one in our respective *wilayas* had heard of us.

Fatiha's delivery was imminent. We decided to go and see Nouara Djaffar, now Minister for the Family. She had promised to help us. This time, we traveled by night: that way, we saved a day and I didn't leave my

34. Government Bureaucracy Merry-Go-Round

children alone for too long. It was also much cheaper. And when the bus stopped so people could buy sandwiches, we pretended to be asleep.

At dawn, the three of us arrived exhausted at the Algiers bus station. But at least we could wash up and have a coffee while waiting for the administration to open.

Nouara Djaffar was scandalized by our situation:

- I'm going to call the Minister of Solidarity today to ask him about the status of your case. Personally, I have no power, I can't help you: my ministry is poor. But I'm also going to tell the *walis*. They must release your housing quickly!

We also tried to contact Khalida Toumi, now Minister of Culture, but to no avail.

We also went back to see the Minister of Solidarity's chief of staff. He seemed astonished by what we were telling him.

- I'll do what's necessary," he assured us.

We left his office with fifty kilos of macaroni.

A few weeks later, we finally received our summons to go to the social services in our *wilayas*: in the absence of housing or work, from now on, every time we went there, we would receive food and sign a discharge. We couldn't refuse this comfort: we were in desperate need of these food resources.

Fatiha, after several requests for an audience, was received by the president of her APC, her baby under one arm and her file under the other.

- Madam, it's true that you've been seriously assaulted, but we can't allocate you accommodation: you're not the head of the family. We can't allocate housing to your husband either, since he's not the one who was attacked. So we can't accept your application.

Their administrative reasoning made us walk on our heads, to the point that Fatiha told me on the phone:

- If I didn't have my child, I'd leave here to be a whore, that's what they're pushing you to! I'm tired of begging.

As for the trial, it was postponed again and again. And with them, our long, pointless journeys and our disappointments.

We waited for hours under the threatening gazes of the accused and their families. They continued to come without lawyers, counting on time to dilute the case. On our side, they still didn't come, despite the promises of the associations.

I've often thought of throwing myself, like a kamikaze, against the walls of the courthouse, armed with dynamite to blow things up.

I've lost count of the number of trips the three of us have made to Algiers, with Fatiha now carrying her baby with her.

34. Government Bureaucracy Merry-Go-Round

Ministry doors often only opened if we threatened to go to the press.

The Minister of Solidarity's chief of staff eventually stopped seeing us and referred us to a colleague of his. We had already met her in Hassi. She had accompanied the minister and his chief of staff. She had cried a lot and swore to us that they wouldn't forget us.

- Where are all those promises you made to us while you were shedding all those tears?" asked Fatiha in a slightly sour voice.

- I'm sorry your situation is so dire. Believe me, if I had the power to help you, I would. Please send my regards to Diar Rahma[17]. Maybe they can do something for you.

She pulled 1,000 dinars from her purse and laid them against Fatiha's baby.

- It's to buy him a little present," she says in a voice full of concern.

But Fatiha wasn't interested in these good feelings that would never get us out of trouble:

- That's not what I'm asking. We want work, housing. We're not begging. Help us get a project. We're not beggars," she snapped.

Nouara Djaffar refused to see us.

---

17. Shelter centers run by the Ministry of Solidarity.

We went so far as to write a letter to the president. We had the other women sign it, begging him to help us. And to finally put an end to this never-ending trial!

We never got an answer.

Perhaps he never even received our request.

Despite all our disappointments, we kept telling ourselves that we had no right to give up. That we had to fight and defend ourselves to the bitter end, so that no woman, assaulted, raped, beaten by her husband, her brother, a stranger or a pack of enraged men, would ever again be afraid to walk through the doors of a courtroom in the hope of obtaining justice and reparation.

It was essential for us to get this message across.

35. The Third Trial

On January 3, 2005, at 8am, Fatiha, Nadia and I turned up for the fifth time at the Biskra court.

We hadn't slept a wink the night before. Nadia had huge bags under her eyes. Fatiha was sickly pale.

The idea of seeing our torturers and their families once again, perhaps for nothing, was more distressing than anything else. In the courthouse lobby, menacing orders were still being issued:

- Forgive! Withdraw your complaints!

But this time, we were not alone: in 2004, Salima Tlemçani had published several articles in the daily *El Watan in* which she defended our cause body and soul. In one of the latter, she pointed the finger at the inertia of the associations. Thanks to her, things had moved on.

We were supported by all the women's associations, the national press and a few foreign journalists. We also recognized many of the people who had visited us at the inn in 2001.

And we had lawyers! Ill-prepared: they'd only had access to our voluminous files for two or three days; but two of them were highly motivated.

There were six defendants. None of them recognized the facts.

It was clear from their profiles that none of them was unemployed or in a precarious situation; yet that's how their defenders had presented them, as if to clear their names.

Among them, I recognized two.

One of their lawyers asked me:

- Since you recognize them, tell us what they did to you.

- They've done the unspeakable," I said softly, my throat dry and my speech slurred.

I was paralyzed, my head was spinning. All these people! How could I tell them about my torn clothes, my lacerated breasts and thighs? And my three children would know all the details!

I couldn't answer, it was beyond my strength. But the lawyer insisted, peremptory and intransigent:

- Tell us exactly what they did to you.

The judge asked the lawyer not to embarrass the victims by asking about the sexual details. Then the lawyer, in his confident voice, said:

- Why do you think they attacked you?

His question was a conclusion, and he turned on his heels without my being able to answer. Faced with his allusions and the humiliation he was inflicting on me, I held back my tears with all the strength I had left.

Fatiha, when summoned in her turn, declared, defiant and full of anger:

- I'll tell you what they did to me!

As she spoke, her body trembled more and more. Her voice rose and rose, and soon it was her rage that exploded through the words, her words of violence, of torture, that she uttered without sparing the assembly anything. Her ordeal, her humiliation; her desire to finally hear the executioners confess. She stared them straight in the eye, pointing at them. She showed her burn marks, urged the judge to look at the photos, to circulate them around the assembly, so that everyone could see, and no one could claim ignorance or innocence.

- From now on, Judge, I no longer live. My husband is a good man, but I asked for a divorce because the idea of a man touching me disgusts me. I feel dirty. Some wounds may have healed, but inside everything is raw. They buried me alive and I spent two hours in the morgue because my heart stopped beating in the ambulance. It was the investigators who got me out when they saw that my fingers were moving. Since then, I've been known as the living dead. And that's how I feel. Dead. They ruined my life!

Her pain was intense. But the words came out. The assembly was overwhelmed.

The judge turned to one of the defendants named in Fatiha's minutes.

- So you still don't know her?

- No, I swear I don't remember ever meeting her," replies the accused without batting an eyelid.

- In any case, she'll remember you and your comrades for the rest of her life," says the judge, handing the man some photos to refresh his memory.

The accused sweated profusely.

- It's not me, it's not me," he repeated, suddenly much less at ease.

Another said:

- I was asleep when it happened. The noise woke me up. I just went out to have a look but, frightened by the crowd, I went straight back in. I haven't slept since these unjust accusations were made against me. I'm traumatized, Judge.

Fatiha raised her hand and exclaimed:

- It's not true, Judge! He was one of my attackers, he tortured me like the others.

The judge then ironically asked a third man if he, too, had not been aware of anything. The presumed one declared:

- Yes, yes, I knew all about it. I heard rumors that our neighborhoods needed to be cleared of brothels. I observed things, but from a distance.

- You weren't that far off, since eleven victims recognized you. Do you know what a brothel is?

- Yes, yes, I've seen them. But in Ouargla, not in Hassi.

The magistrates and the audience couldn't help but laugh.

A fourth said he had very poor eyesight and always had to get home before dark: how could he have taken part in the massacre?

We were shocked that none of the accused confessed, and we wept at their contempt and the calmness with which they made their statements.

The public prosecutor's closing argument put a smile on our faces:

- The acts for which we are gathered here today are a disgrace to Algeria as a whole, and take us back to the Stone Age. On that dark night of July 13, 2001, Algerian women were terribly violated in the name of Islam. No Muslim on earth can accept or tolerate such barbaric acts. For this, justice demands the most severe punishment, commensurate with this savagery and cruelty. The fact that the other victims are not here today in no way diminishes the guilt of the accused.

The jury retired to deliberate. After three hours, the verdict was delivered and the sentences announced:

Criminal imprisonment for the absent defendants :

In absentia, 20 sentences to 20 years' imprisonment, 4 sentences to 10 years' imprisonment, 1 sentence to 5 years' imprisonment.

Criminal sentences for the defendants present: 1 sentenced to 8 years, 1 to 6 years and the third to 3 years. And 3 acquittals.

Each convict had to pay us 100,000 dinars in compensation. But how could they? They weren't solvent.

The man in the grey shirt and patched sandals who tortured Fatiha has been cleared.

The man with the red bandana, who had tried to decapitate Fatiha, who had raped her, who had raped Nadia and so many other women, torn my clothes and stabbed me, he was the one who had only 8 years in prison.

The acquittals were due to the absence of the thirty-seven other victims.

Fatiha was upset by the verdict and very angry. She screamed at the top of her voice in the court hall:

- I don't want your money, I want my lost honor and dignity back! I want justice! I want the newspaper that portrayed us as prostitutes to right its wrong!

We were all deeply moved, our wounds still raw, our tears still burning.

I couldn't help thinking about the day they'd get out: what if they tried to find us? The monstrous acts they had committed proved to us that they were capable of it.

And the contumacious ones were still running...

That night, in the city, we heard sounds of demonstrations.

We were terrified that it might be because of us.

36. Between the taxiphone and the law

On January 6, Fatiha, Nadia and I went to the Ministry of Solidarity, along with three other victims who had attended the trial. Halim, the director, had encouraged us:

- Don't miss your chance, it's now or never to apply. It's now or never that you'll be heard.

We were accompanied by all the association representatives. This huge mobilization warmed our hearts.

We were greeted and congratulated by the Director General of the Ministry of Solidarity, the Deputy Director of the Department of Social Action (DAS) and the Director of Angem.

I began by asking that the addresses of the victims no longer appear on the judgment, so that the culprits couldn't find them. Then, together, we told them that we wanted to set up a taxiphone project, through which we hoped to provide for our families.

The idea met with unanimous approval.

Ms Seddaoui, the director of the DAS, urged us to put together files and hand them over to her as soon as possible; she wanted to support our candidacy in our respective *wilayas*, as part of a campaign entitled "One hundred premises per *wilaya*". Enthusiastically, we brought them to her a few days after the meeting.

For his part, the general manager offered us a microcredit of 27,000 dinars (270 euros). But one of us pointed out that any association, no matter how poor, could have raised such a small sum for us. We expected something else from them.

Ms Seddaoui reassured us that the authorization to open lines is usually very complicated to obtain.

As we were leaving the meeting, the president of Afepec, an association based in western Algeria, tried to convince us to overturn the ruling.

I refused. I didn't want to be informed of my trial at the last minute, to have to travel all over Algeria to get to court, or to be subjected to further pressure from prisoners and their families. I didn't want to end up with lawyers who were ill-prepared or absent altogether. I didn't want to travel to hear that the trial had been postponed. Just thinking about it was devastating.

I wanted to move on. To put all my strength, all my energy into this project that would enable me and my family to get out of this life of misery. Perhaps it was

36. Between the taxiphone and the law

the energy of despair, the last strength of a drowning man who sees the shore. I threw myself into the race to stay afloat.

But Fatiha was persuaded. She overturned the judgment.

As promised by Ms Seddaoui, each of us received a convocation from our respective *wilaya*. Unfortunately, the local Hundreds for each *wilaya* had already been distributed. We would have to wait two years to benefit from this campaign. None of us had a job. It was impossible to hold out until then. I insisted on knowing if there were any other premises available outside the program. I was assured that there were not.

No matter, I'd break up my apartment and turn it into a room: to provide for my family, that was all I needed.

I soon learned that our addresses had not been removed from the judgments. It made my hair stand on end: facing our executioners, we weren't even entitled to that kind of protection!

I called the Ministry of Solidarity. I was told that there was nothing they could do, and that I would have to make arrangements directly with my local *wilaya*. So I made a request in writing, setting out my fears, with the help of a cousin who drew up the letter for me (I couldn't go to my children, as the story would have frightened them). It bothers me to depend on people when it comes to writing something down and to have to lay out my life in front of them, but I left school so early and my handwriting is so bad!

As far as the taxiphone was concerned, the president of the APC, whom I'd been pestering, told me that I had to apply to Opgi to convert my two-room flat into premises. The deputy director of the DAS then put me in touch with a regional manager of the DAS in Oran to help me with my application to the Opgi. I have to say that he spared no effort, calling them again and again until they gave me the authorization I needed.

The PTT company came to dig the line, which cost us 24,000 dinars, even though we didn't even have the computer or communications equipment yet, and I hadn't even broken the wall of my apartment! Fatiha and I preferred to laugh at this gag.

But when I asked the president of the APC for financial support for my work, he would have none of it. And all my family members tried to dissuade me when I told them I needed money for the project:

- You only have a two-room apartment. Where will you sleep?

- Not a problem," I replied. After closing time, I'll give it a quick wipe and it'll be my room. As you can see, I have no choice.

36. Between the taxiphone and the law

In the end, it was my niece's husband who agreed to lend me the money.

In all, my work cost me 250,000 dinars. This sum, enormous for me - and a far cry from the 27,000-dinar microcredit granted by the Director General of the Ministry of Solidarity, which I also had to repay - gave me cold sweats. I couldn't sleep a wink. How could I pay back all that money? I didn't even have the taxiphone equipment yet! And the estimate Fatiha and I drew up for computers, telephones, etc. came to 60,000 dinars...

- I don't have anyone to lend me that kind of money," Fatiha told me in despair, all the more so because, like me, she had started work to transform her house into a shop.

- And I've exhausted everyone with my loan applications," I replied.

But there was no turning back.

We returned to Algiers to ask for help. The Director General of the Ministry of Solidarity refused to support us:

- There are thirty-nine victims. If I help both of you, I'm showing favoritism. So either I help all thirty-nine, or none at all.

- Start by helping us, and you'll see that all the others will follow.

So we went to Darna, where the president of Rachda told us:

- I'm willing to help you, but it'll be a loan with an IOU that you'll sign before a notary: 92,500 dinars plus 3,000 dinars in notary fees. You'll have to pay me back this sum within two years.

Fatiha was absolutely furious:

- Everyone says that any business is only profitable after three years. We demanded nothing in return when you made your documentaries about us! And without ever asking our opinion, you published a book with nude photos of us that were only intended for the courts! It was humiliating, but then again, we didn't dare reproach you. Do you think that made us happy?

But she was our only recourse. What else could we do? We had to accept her conditions: we signed the IOU with a notary and paid 3,000 dinars. We submitted ourselves, heartbroken and shocked; but we were able to buy the equipment we needed for our business.

All these debts were giving me a real headache.
It was absolutely essential to make this business work.
We opened the taxiphone.
My son helped me run the business and, after a few months, the results were quite positive: we were located just a few meters from a bus stop and customers were flocking in. I was thrilled, life was brightening up and the future was looking brighter at last.

36. Between the taxiphone and the law

To my surprise, Youssef would drop by the taxiphone to see my son when I wasn't around. Even
though we still didn't speak, these little visits eased
my resentment.

After a year, we began to get huge bills that didn't
correspond to outgoing calls from the taxiphone. We
soon discovered that our line was being hijacked:
when we picked up the phones, we heard the sounds
of interfering voices; their conversations were at our
expense.

Despite our numerous complaints, the PTT refused
to open an investigation and ordered us to pay the bills.

And soon we suffered another blow to our small
business and our wobbly means: in 2006, at the same
time as the abundance of cell phones, a new pheno-
menon appeared, "flixing", thanks to which you could
charge units on your cell phone from anywhere. This
was a huge success, and put the cab companies in
financial difficulties.

I could no longer pay my rent and found myself
a year in arrears. I also stopped paying my water and
telephone bills. As for my debts, I had barely begun
to repay them: under threat from the bailiffs, I had
already paid back half of the 27,000-dinar microcredit.

The president of the Femmes en détresse association
soon came to my aid. She paid all my Opgi arrears,

my water bills and part of my PTT. This woman has always supported us.

But our attempt to escape our misery was doomed, much to my despair. I'd broken the wall of my apartment for nothing. What was left but my children, who had never known material comfort or the comfort of having a close-knit family around them?

37. Trial in Absentia

I regularly called the court in Biskra to find out how our trial was progressing, since we had finally applied for an appeal to the Supreme Court. But on May 15, 2006, I was told that a person in absentia was to be tried without delay.

An association sent us two eminent lawyers from eastern Algeria, who did not receive our files until two days before the trial.

We still had to swallow the miles of dust to endure the threats and intimidation of the accused, to exhaust ourselves on the stand in our memories, to listen to ill-prepared lawyers who claimed to be defending us.

Was it worth it?

The evening before, at the hotel, I met our two lawyers. Maîtres Boutamine and Soudani. Of course, they would have prepared the case better if they'd had more time; very kindly, they assured me of their support while understanding our decision.

- If, later on, you want to take over the business, we'll be there, they told me.

Why didn't we meet them sooner?

We told the judge we wanted to postpone the trial.

The in absentia convict was released on the spot.

But what would we do the next time? Would we have to travel dozens and dozens of kilometers to face our executioners without the slightest protection? It was unthinkable.

38. *Moussalaha*[18]

We landed in Hassi on a cool winter's morning, just as the muezzins were calling the Fajr prayer. The cold bit into our bodies and fear twisted our guts.

We went straight to the police station and waited an eternity to be received by the commissioner. He had been informed of our arrival by the head of the Human Rights Observatory, Mr. Boucetta, whom we had visited in Algiers. He found our idea excellent and generous. What's more, it would satisfy the President.

The superintendent called the imam of Hassi's main mosque to ask for our permission to come to his house.

When he saw us, he realized just how much this was costing us: Fatiha choked on her sobs every time she tried to open her mouth.

---

18. Reconciliation.

I said to the imam:

- Even if we can't forget, we want to forgive so that we're no longer afraid that an absentee will find us and execute us. We don't want any more women to suffer threats or reprisals because of our convictions, so that we can return to a semblance of normal life. We want to forgive so that one day we won't be afraid to return to Hassi. And if we don't come back, our children will, because our families have to survive. Then, as the President says: there can be no peace without reconciliation, there can be no reconciliation without forgiveness. Is it possible to meet the families of the contumacious?

- We're going to try and contact the families of the contumacious. I have to go to Mecca, but when I get back, we'll organize a meeting with them. I'll say during my Friday sermon that you are women of honor.

The convicts' families refused to meet us.

- Why should they forgive our children? They haven't done anything! We don't need their forgiveness. Our sons are innocent.

They would continue to deny the facts. But also to humiliate us.

We were very bitter.

We didn't get the status of "victims of terrorism" we were promised at Human Rights.

But if we were to count the promises made to us since our lynching...

Today, when I go to the *wilaya* or Diar Rahma, I don't even try to ask for a job or housing, I ask for food. Lentils, dried beans, cans of sardines.

I find myself dreaming that every foreign or Algerian oil company that had employed a woman victim had paid us the defense fees for a lawyer to have a real trial.

I can't help dreaming that the women's associations, with their strength in numbers, knowledge and education, but also their fighting traditions, would have stood by us steadfastly throughout this long legal battle.

I find myself dreaming that the promises made by the various ministers had been kept.

That we had finally had a landmark trial. An exemplary trial. And since then, no woman has been afraid to face our country's justice system...

But as they say, one hand does not clap.

The imam of El Haïcha is now imam of a larger mosque on one of Hassi's main boulevards.

My brother Youssef died after a long illness. When I visited him in hospital, knowing he was dying, he turned his gaze towards me, painful, so painful... Then he passed away.

Fatiha and Ayachi have had their second child. They named her Amal, meaning "hope". Ayachi finally found work as a night watchman, one hundred and twenty kilometers from home. A fixed-term contract.

Hamid, my boy, does a steady stream of odd jobs while waiting to burn the border, as he puts it.

My daughter Nacéra will soon be a hairdresser. She is assiduously following her CAP.

Soon, Hassina, my youngest daughter, will pass her baccalaureate. She'll be off to university.

Soon I'll be going back to Hassi.

Epilogue

How Persasive Machismo veers into Barbarism

When I was a child in Algiers, when I wasn't at school learning from my textbook, when little Malik was playing soccer and little Zina was washing the dishes, I accompanied my mother wherever she went. In this way, she hoped to protect herself from the harassment she experienced in the street. This method wasn't always effective. I remember once, a man followed us for a good kilometer, whispering insanities to Mom as he jingled his car keys. Exasperated, my mother complained to a traffic policeman.

- Why are you saying this to me? I'm not your husband!" replied the cop.

On another occasion, on a bus, as an elderly man was starting to cling to her, my mother hit him with a bag full of yoghurts purchased at the cost of a very long wait in a downtown *souk el fellah*[19]. While our rare commodity, which had splashed onto a few annoyed or even amused travellers, dripped down the lecherous old man's face, the bus driver dropped us off at the first police station.

- At your age...," reproached the superintendent to the old man!

I was surprised that he didn't blame her for what she'd done, but rather for her age.

A few years later, policemen with German shepherds appeared in town. They checked couples and rounded up unmarried couples and girls not dressed to their liking. These were called "hygiene and sanitation campaigns". My classmate, who at the time was 11 years old and a head taller than us, found herself in a salad basket because she was wearing red overalls that we all envied, and that the police deemed too tight-fitting. We laughed at this anecdote, but it also saddened us, because it was a shock to our childhood.

Surprisingly, the police never worried the stalkers.

---

19. The *souks el Fellah*, also known as Algerian galleries, were state-run stores. In those days of scarcity, people had to queue for long hours before hoping to be served.

How Persasive Machismo veers into Barbarism

In those days, it was not uncommon for men in the street to come to the rescue of young girls or women who were being harassed.

In 1984, just as I was emerging from adolescence, where I was still learning, like all the other girls, that moving around in the public space accompanied by constant harassment that didn't say its name was not an easy exercise, a majority of deputies in the National Assembly voted for a series of articles of law that codified the couple's relationship within marriage and the family, including inheritance. The Family Code. With horror, we discovered the personal status of women. A minor for life, she passed from father to husband and owed obedience to her husband[20]. Polygamy was recognized, and men could marry up to four women, if they so wished[21]. Women did not have the right to divorce, nor did they have parental authority over their own children[22]. However, she could be repudiated at any time[23]. It was impossible for a Muslim woman to marry a non-Muslim[24]. Inheritance between men and women was unequal[25]. The husband had the

---

20. Article 39 of the Family Code.
21. Art. 8.
22. Art. 53.
23. Art. 48.
24. Art. 31.
25. Art. 126, art. 183.

right to keep the marital home[26], the guardianship of the children and to make his entire family homeless. Before long, women and their children were begging and sleeping rough all over town.

This code instituted the superiority of men over women, legalized injustice and, by placing women and their children at risk, undermined society as a whole.

Years of relentless struggle by feminist movements and democrats (who were greatly weakened during the terrorist period) to denounce this code came to nothing. Then, after an unprecedented media campaign launched by the association 20 ans barakat[27], led by some thirty women's associations in France and Algeria between 2002 and 2005[28], the Family Code was finally overhauled and several of the most discriminatory articles concerning the duty of obedience, divorce, housing after divorce and paternal guardianship of children were repealed.

Unfortunately, the damage had already been done.

This code, which officially places women at the disposal and under the control of men, is, for me, one of the factors that made possible the lynching of the women of Hassi Messaoud in 2001.

---

26. Art. 52.

27. (20 years is enough.)

28. All these associations have formed a collective also called 20 ans barakat.

The second important factor is the far-reaching work of fundamentalists who, for years, have permeated every fabric of society with their deeply misogynistic, unequal discourse between men and women. Constantly blaming women when they demanded their rights, making them responsible for all the ills of society, they twisted religious texts in favor of men, thereby reinforcing their supremacy.

During the years of triumphant terrorism, in addition to the insulting, threatening rhetoric shouted from minarets all over the country, thousands of women were kidnapped by fundamentalist armed groups. They were raped, tortured and enslaved. Many of them were murdered or disappeared into thin air.

Their executioners, now known as *"repenters"* (without actually having repented of anything), were never - or very rarely - questioned.

Today, mosque loudspeakers can rant the same insults and threats against women without ever being sued for defamation or incitement to hatred.

And, as a sign of the violence with which society is steeped - *a fortiori* a society whose various institutions (educational, legislative, religious...) allow women to be denigrated on a daily basis - violence against women has increased alarmingly. Rape and kidnapping are unfortunately high on the list, and still not punished enough, as was the case in Oran in October 2009, where a man who had raped eleven women was sentenced to five years in prison.

Fortunately, a good number of women's rights and human rights defenders are working tirelessly in the field, mobilizing to re-educate children and young people - children of the ash years - in self-respect, respect for others and the values of equality between men and women. It's an arduous task, since they have far fewer resources than the fundamentalists, and progressive readings of religious texts - which are today the primary reference point in society - are not as fashionable as those that promote hatred of the other and the different.

Others - or the same ones - are working to change the laws, to do away with discrimination in the Family Code and reservations to the International Convention on the Elimination of All Forms of Discrimination against Women...

We have a long way to go before there is another Hassi Messaoud.

Nadia Kaci

Aknowledgments

Thanks to Louisa AÎT HAMOU, member of the Wassila network, who enabled us to meet, and for her listening and advice; thanks to Malika LAÎCHOUR; Salima BENHOUHOU; Caroline BRAC DE LA PERRIÈRE; Nadia LYASSINE, President of the 20 ans barakat association; Samia ALLALOU; Mounès KHAMAR; Dalila LAMARÈNE-DJERBAL, sociologist, member of the Wassila network; Meriem BELLALA, President of the SOS-femmes en détresse association; Halim SAHRAOUI and Karine BOUCHAMA.

Table of contents

Best sellers Max Milo Editions

Hitler's banker, Jean-François Bouchard

Confessions of a forger, Éric Piedoie Le Tiec

The Koran and the flesh, Ludovic-Mohamed Zahed

Governing by fake news, Jacques Baud

Governing by chaos, Collectif

A political history of food, Paul Ariès

Mad in U.S.A.: The ravages of the "American model",
Michel Desmurget

Mondial soccer club geopolitics, Kévin Veyssière

Putin: Game master?, Jacques Braud

Treatise on the three impostors: Moses, Jesus, Muhammad,
The Spirit of Spinoza

TV Lobotomy, Michel Desmurget